Notes from Mama

DAWN HOWARD

WESTBOW
PRESS®
A DIVISION OF THOMAS NELSON
& ZONDERVAN

WestBow Press books may be ordered through booksellers or by contacting:

WestBow Press
A Division of Thomas Nelson & Zondervan
1663 Liberty Drive
Bloomington, IN 47403
www.westbowpress.com
844-714-3454

ISBN: 978-1-6642-2939-6 (sc)
ISBN: 978-1-6642-2941-9 (hc)
ISBN: 978-1-6642-2940-2 (e)

Library of Congress Control Number: 2021906605

Print information available on the last page.

WestBow Press rev. date: 5/14/2021

This book is dedicated to my husband and children.

with finite minds, can't begin to understand the infinite no matter how hard we try. Through it all, we need to remember that we are created in the image and likeness of our Creator and that He holds us in His mighty hand. May you receive peace and understanding and learn the truth in the words that are written as the Spirit guides my heart, mind, and hand.

1

Blessings

JANUARY 16, 2020

Blessed is he who comes in the name of the Lord.
—Psalm 118:26 (NIV)

As I thought of the title for this book, this verse automatically came to me. That's quite strange because I didn't know whether it even was a verse, but sure enough it is. That's how the Spirit can work in our lives if we allow it to. As usual, my Lord always points me to which book I should pick up in the morning. It can vary, but they are all about God's Word. This morning, I was prompted to pick up the *Upper Room*[1] and read "Casting Our Nets" written by Andrew Garland Breeden. I very rarely have the opportunity to read the devotionals in this magazine; however, the church that I am now attending provides it.

I opened the magazine to the middle, where one of the editors had written about routines and the fact that he was a routine person. He further went on to explain that routines can put us into ruts and

---

[1] *Upper Room*, January–February 2020, 40–41: This material is reprinted from The Upper Room magazine, copyright (year) by The Upper Room, Inc., P.O. Box 340004, Nashville, TN 37203-0004, www.upperroom.org, and is used by permission of the publisher.

limit our opportunities. He wrote about the scripture where several of the disciples were fishing and were unable to catch fish. Jesus told them to cast the nets on the other side of the boat. After they did, the fish in their nets were so plentiful that they were unable to haul the catch into their boat. The disciples simply changed the side on which they cast their nets, which got them out of their usual routine and the rut.

I thought of my husband and myself after reading about routines. In the past couple of weeks, we have moved away from thinking the same old thoughts, and as a result, we are being blessed. God blesses us so that we can bless others. The devil sure has been trying to get in the way, but we are fighting hard to resist him and his demons. We know that the angels sent by God are armored and fighting as well.

We need to list our blessings so that, whenever we get down in the mouth and begin to complain, we can be reminded of God's goodness. Every morning we need to wake up and thank God for our night's rest before jumping out of bed. Prayer is talking with God, the Son, and the Holy Spirit. It is talking with the Trinity, not only in a silent manner but speaking the words as well.

I am notorious for talking to myself and even answering myself. Now, I tend to talk with God and Jesus when I need to express my emotions and upsets. We don't need to grumble to others. We should take our grievances to Jesus so that He can give us a better perspective on the matter. I am reminded of the Israelites as they wandered in the wilderness for forty years because of their disobedience and their grumbling. God would provide, they would rejoice, and then they would begin to grumble again. That's not unlike many of us, including myself. There is no one on this planet to whom you can turn for the guidance, direction, calmness, and provisions of God. He is always with us. This is a difficult concept for us to understand as humans. The more we focus on the face of Jesus, study and meditate on the Word, and communicate with the Father, Son, and Holy Spirit, the more that our eyes will be opened to the truth. Jesus said, "The truth will set you free" (John 8:32 NLT).

Even though the devil has tried over and over again to interrupt my process of submitting my manuscript to the publishers, my focus is on the eyes and face of Jesus as He stands beside me to guide me and to bless me and my husband. May the Lord bless you too so that, in turn, you can bless others.

2

Christmas

DECEMBER 23, 2018

> She gave birth to her first child, a son. She wrapped
> him snugly in strips of cloth and laid him in a manger,
> because there was no lodging available for them.
> —Luke 2:7 (NLT)

Jesus, the Savior of the world, came into this world without the pomp and circumstance that an earthly king would have received. As I sit and look upon my Charlie Brown Christmas tree, the lights remind me that Jesus is the light of the world. The evergreen leaves remind me of His promise of everlasting life if we accept and believe in Him. The ornaments remind me of the gifts brought to the newborn king by the wise men. The angel that sits atop the tree reminds me of the proclamation and the songs of the heavenly hosts who appeared before the shepherds tending to their sheep out in the field at night.

The memories that I want to create now will focus on the real meaning of Christmas—time to share with family and friends, to prepare special food, and to engage in other activities such as making gingerbread houses, driving through neighborhoods looking at Christmas lights, and having family gatherings in anticipation of the coming day. Jesus wasn't bombarded with gifts. In fact, Mary and Joseph didn't even expect gifts to be given to their baby. However, God knew that His child would be sought after by King Herod, and God provided the means for escape to Egypt more than likely through the use of the gifts given by the wise men.

If Jesus had just received three gifts, why do we think that we have to provide an unlimited number of gifts to our children and grandchildren each Christmas Day? Have we become more like the world than like the Savior? Do our children and grandchildren come to expect the same unlimited number of gifts each year? What actions of ours leave permanent memories with them? Do they remember the frustrations that we express, the negative thoughts and actions, and the chaos that can be witnessed at Christmastime?

I want to begin a tradition of making kindness, love, sharing, and caring for one another evident and a permanent memory impressed upon each mind—a memory that is not forgotten with the opening and laying aside of each Christmas gift. This would make for a simpler Christmas, not unlike the first Christmas, that begins with the sights, smells, and sharing that culminates with the celebration of the birth of the Savior.

Let there be peace on earth and let it begin with me. This is a good reminder to take with us today, tomorrow, and always.

3

Come

WEDNESDAY, JANUARY 8, 2019

O God, you are my God; I earnestly search for you. My
soul thirsts for you; my whole body longs for you in this
parched and weary land where there is no water.
—Ps. 63:1 (NLT)

David wrote this psalm as he was remembering being in the
wilderness of Judah. I can imagine that the day was hot, the earth
was dry, and he had no water to quench his thirst. But he did have
God. He felt the presence, and he knew that God was near even
though he was desperately trying to find Him. One has to ask, Why
was David so close to God's heart, and why was David so precious
to Him? Could it be that David just laid everything out to Him in
pure honesty? Could it be that David trusted that God would take
care of him as he had so many times in the past? Could it be that
David had a heart like a child? What makes us wonder and think
that this isn't or couldn't be the case for us? What makes us distance
ourselves from the One who created us?

Many today may not have even been introduced to the Word of
God. I think that most have heard about God, Christ, and the Holy
Spirit, but do they really know and understand who the Trinity is? I

was introduced to the community of believers before I was even born because my mother and father attended church. I am a daughter of two ordained ministers. I knew about Jesus before I could talk. My own children were also brought up in the church; however, I was not as faithful as I should have been, and it is reflected in my life. Despite this, God did not leave me; I distanced myself from Him. He has always been with me, but He stepped back to let me try to find the path on my own; I failed miserably until I searched earnestly for Him as David did in the wilderness.

We may not be in a physical wilderness, but we have our physical, emotional, mental, and even social wildernesses. At least I know to search earnestly for God, but so many others don't know how. I am struggling with the next step in my life. I have finally realized, a little too late, that I can't physically do what I have done in the past. I had a wonderful career, but I complained about it often and finally said *enough*. But I didn't prepare for the next step. I got distracted, procrastinated, and have been lazy. Why? I could make excuses, but I might as well fess up. I learned a long time ago to quit making excuses and blaming others and to take responsibility for my own actions. I can't fix things for others, as I have tried to do over and over again as a nurturing caregiver. I can't change someone's mind or even begin to know that person's mind. I can focus only on myself and where God wants me to go.

I keep hearing the voice from within to finish this book, which I have once again put on the back burner for many reasons. I could submit this manuscript in a week if I just focused on it. It's not like I don't have lots of other journals to pull from. God is going to get through to me in one way or another when it comes to my stubbornness. He is going to set me straight before I enter the pearly gates of heaven. He is going to remind me over and over again why I was sent here at this specific time in history and the purpose for which I was sent. He allows me to freely make choices, and I understand that there are consequences for my actions or lack thereof. I am not alone and never have been. I know it as time to

"Seven periods of time will pass while you live this way, until you learn that the Most High rules over the kingdoms of the world and gives them to anyone he chooses" (Daniel 4: 25 NLT). Even though Daniel was talking with the king of Babylon at the time, telling the king that he would roam in the fields "like a cow" for seven years until he realized that God is in control of everything, can the verse not also remind me of the same? I might not literally roam in the fields for seven years, but if I refuse to do what God has asked me to do, I may have a dry spell until I am willing to accept that I don't control anything in my life and that I have to trust and obey the directions given to me by Christ.

So, as my husband often says, do I sit on the fence, be indecisive, continue to be like a boat with the waves tossing me about, and see a storm approaching but refuse to prepare? Or do I move forward, get off the fence, make a decision—whether it's right or wrong—and use my "rudder" to control the direction that I steer on the waves as I prepare for the storm? What makes me this way? Does it matter? Shouldn't I recognize it for what it is and deal with it? The one thing I do know is that I should move forward and move now. I can't continue to look back and think, *I wonder what it would have been like if I had done this?* I can't look in the future and say, "It's going to happen this way." Jesus reminds us to focus on today. He tells us that we have enough to worry about for today—not yesterday, not tomorrow, but today. It's a matter of doing what He tells us to do when He tells us to do it and remembering that God controls it all. God puts each of us here, at this specific time in history, born to specific parents, for He has a unique calling for each of us. I am reminded of the verse, "I can do all things through him who strengthens me" (Philippians 4:13 ESV). We just have to make up our minds and do it.

I can't advise you on how to handle your problems. But I can listen as you vent. I can pray for intervention, for relief from God. Could it be as simple as accepting the truth that, until you learn that the Most High rules over the kingdoms of the world and gives them to anyone he chooses, your life will change? Dare to be a Daniel. Dare to stand up to oppression that can attack your mind. Dare to move full-steam ahead.

5

Emotionally Drained

OCTOBER 5, 2012

I cannot do anything on my own.
—John 5:30 (CEV)

Christ said that He couldn't do anything on His own without the Father, so why do we arrogantly think we can do things on our own? Our life experiences can cause us a lot of problems, affecting the way we think and the way we express ourselves to others. We need to be examples to those around us. This is so hard to do. I am thankful that each of you are kind to people. Every time we make a cruel comment about someone, we most certainly pierce the heart of Christ and put another stripe on His back. All of us can be quick to anger, some more than others, but Christ empowers us, gives us courage to carry on, and wants us to love our brothers and sisters. Christ wants us to show others the warmth of fellowship.

I worked last night at the church with homeless families. I can't even imagine the way that they must feel. They can't provide for their children, they don't have a place to call home, and they have to move every week to a different church. Our purpose is to uplift them, encourage them, and praise them for their abilities, for each person has a talent. I have been helping during mealtime. I know that I will be very tired when I get home because I have been for the past two nights. It takes an emotional toll on my being.

I can't even begin to imagine how Christ felt after being with the crowds for hours on end, teaching them as much as possible within the three years of His ministry. It's no wonder that He went off by Himself to rest and pray. I'm sure that His human nature required and needed encouragement and strength from Our Father. Christ knew His mission. Just as I am tired, I too will pray that God will give me the strength to carry on. I am not only physically drained but emotionally drained. May the Lord bless you and keep each of you safe and strong.

6

Encouragement

TUESDAY, JANUARY 21, 2020

The lord is a shelter for the oppressed,
a refuge in times of trouble.
—Psalm 9:9 (NLT)

I sit at the desk in the office of our house as darkness surrounds the world. I am up while most are sleeping, though many will be getting up soon to prepare for the day. I have once again been reminded that God is closer than we think. We are the ones who run from Him. God doesn't turn His back on us.

Yesterday, we received word that the older couple who had promised with a handshake to rent our home beginning in May has decided not to do so. It seemed that God had answered our prayer before we had even spoken it. One has to remember that God opens doors when other doors are shut. We don't know the workings of God, but we need to trust that He has a better plan. We may not ever know the couple's reasoning for backing out; all we can do is take them at their word. Even though they had expressed a desire to rent this house for two years, all can change in a twinkling of an eye. While they looked at the house, I thought about what could happen. So did they back out because I didn't trust God? No, it is the reality of the situation. If one starts to think of the reality, then one begins to realize that the possibility of the reality may, in fact, be the truth. This couple may have changed their minds, but I know that God has another family in mind for this house. He knows our needs well before we know them ourselves.

We were disappointed yesterday. We were even angry, and for me to deny that emotion would be untrue. We felt defeated. We had told others and had begun to make other plans for our relocation to another place. We thought that we were in control. Just when we think that we are in control, God makes us realize that we aren't. We just have to wait patiently for Him to answer. It doesn't mean that we sit back and do nothing; it means that we work to the best of our ability each and every day.

If nothing else comes of this couple's interest, I talked with the wife at length about visiting the church that we attend. She said that they had not been able to find a church where they felt comfortable since their move to this area. I wrote down the name, address, and phone number and gave it to her. We were able to connect with this couple, but isn't that what we are directed to do? Church is not a building but a gathering of faith believing people. Church doesn't just happen on Sundays but should be every day. When two or more are gathered in His name, there He is also. It is a time for us to search for the truth, for the truth will set us free.

When we encounter disappointments in life, our human nature encourages us to blame and lash out at those who love us unconditionally. Instead, we should turn to God in prayer for guidance and continued patience. Just as soldiers march onward, we must march onward for then we will see the light at the end of the tunnel. Once we are close, we won't want to turn back but move closer to the "light".

I have taped to my laptop the Prayer of Jabez (1 Chronicles 4:10), for it reminds me that God grants what we ask for in His time and not our own. We ask that God bless us, enlarge our territory, be with us, protect us from evil, and not cause pain to others—a good reminder for me this morning.

7

Feeding of the Five Thousand

OCTOBER 19, 2018

> And He said to them, "Come aside by
> yourselves to a deserted place and rest a while'.
> For there were many coming and going,
> and they did not even have time to eat."
> —Mark 6:31 (NKJV)

I was taught about the feeding of the five thousand in Sunday school as a small child. Jesus took two fish and five loaves of bread and fed the multitude who had followed Him and His disciples. Despite being taught about the miracle many times, I don't remember why the five thousand were in the desert. This is why it is important to read the miracle in the context of the chapter and even the preceding chapter—to grasp the reason. The apostles had been sent out by Christ to minister, cast out demons, and heal people as they traveled. They had returned and begun to tell Christ of their journey and that John the Baptist had been beheaded by Herod. Jesus saw the need for His twelve apostles and Himself to withdraw to talk, rest, and eat. They got on a boat, but people who knew Jesus and where He and the twelve might be headed arrived before Jesus and the twelve. Jesus had pity on them and could not turn the five thousand away.

Now, in reality, there were more than five thousand people, as this number does not include women and children.

The crowd sat down and listened to the teachings of Christ. I am sure that Christ gave them hope just as He gives us hope today. We don't read of His blessing, healing, or excising of demons that day, but He taught and performed a miracle. When we read the Bible, we read of many miracles performed by Christ, and I wonder if that makes us think that a miracle has to be "big" to be classified as a miracle. Miracles can also be small blessings from our Father, the Son, and the Holy Spirit, just as I count it a miracle that I slept pain free during the night after a hard day of work. I heard the small voice of Jesus telling me that, when I asked, He would keep me pain free during the night. I am convinced that I slept because of my belief that He would do as He whispered in my ear before bedtime. My pain was almost unbearable when I laid down in my bed even though I had taken pain medication about an hour earlier; in fact, the pain drove me to lay down.

As nighttime approached, the disciples reminded Jesus that the crowd would need to go to villages in the distance to find nourishment since they were in a remote area. After the people had eaten the fish and the loaves, Jesus directed the disciples to get into a boat to cross over to the other side of the sea while Jesus sent the crowd away. We know that Jesus had compassion on the twelve for He knew that they needed to be refreshed after their long journey. Is it possible that Jesus needed to withdraw too because he had just learned that His cousin had been beheaded? There is no doubt that we feel the pain of the death of a close relative.

I lost two cousins at an early age. The one with whom I grew up and knew the most died at the age of nineteen. I had just finished college, as I was about three years older than this cousin. At his funeral, I was in such anguish over this loss that my older and middle brothers had to comfort me. I felt at the time that it should have been me because I had been like the prodigal son, but I was the daughter returning home. I couldn't grasp how God could take my beloved cousin. His life so impacted our lives that my middle brother named his only son for him. Looking back, now I can understand that God has a purpose and an appointed time for each of us to come face to face with Him.

If I was so affected by the loss of my cousin, it seems impossible that Jesus would not feel the loss of His cousin, John. John died a horrific death by having his head chopped off and presented to Herod's wife. I can't even begin to understand how his mother, Elizabeth, handled the pain. This was her only son, whom she had borne as an elderly woman. It is understandable that Jesus would want some alone time to remember his cousin.

If we have faith, then we begin to see the small miracles in life that we otherwise might miss because we are always looking for the "big" miracles. The devil likes to get in the mix of it all, and the evil one would have liked for me to blame God last night for my pain. Yes, we can cry out to God in pain, but we have to also understand that He doesn't create the pain. God knows our pain even before we experience it. You might ask, "Who creates the pain?" Could it be due to our misuse of our earthly bodies? Ponder on that thought. May the Lord bless you throughout the day as He blessed me with a good night's sleep.

8

Fight the Good Fight

NOVEMBER 19, 2019

I pray that God, the source of hope, will fill you
completely with joy and peace because you trust
in him. Then you will overflow with confident
hope through the power of the Holy Spirit.
—Romans 15:13 (NLT)

I sit on the front porch of our house as the storm clouds roll in with
the wind. The breeze feels cool on my arms, but I am so glad to be
in this moment with my Maker. I won't always be on this earth, but
at this moment I want to log this picture within my mind. God does
give us hope through the fact that He gave His only Son to die for
our sins and be victorious over the grave. As we will each lay in a
grave, all in the grave will be on the same level. The graveyard will
contain rich, poor, orphans, widows, men, women, slaves, children,
adults, teens, and many more that have gone on before or will come
after us. In God's eyes, all His children are on the same level too.
He doesn't count one better than another. He looks at us as equals.
That in itself should give us hope. Hope brings light to our eyes and
makes us realize the possibilities that God puts around us. Difficult
times are always there. What matters is how we choose to approach

and live in the difficult times. We think that life is ending, but really it is an opportunity for health, renewal, and growth. As we begin to climb the mountain from the valley, feelings of hope increase as we get closer to the mountaintop.

In a few weeks, I will be undergoing surgery to replace a joint in my knee, which is hurting because bone is rubbing on bone. Yes, I know that there will be pain and that I will need patience as God heals me. A year ago at this time, I was struggling with whether to go back to work or remain at home. I had specific reasons for my return to work after being away for several years—mainly to allow my mind to be renewed. God gave me the desire of my heart, but He also knew that my knee joint would need to be replaced. He knew that my husband would be recovering from his second heart stent placement, that he would have blood clots in his lungs, and that he would almost cut his thumb off with a table saw while taking blood thinners. He knew that my parents would be ill. He knew that I was suffering from emotional distress. He knew it all. He has provided for me. He will continue to provide for me as I move forward in this life. God has always provided for me. He has sent angels when I have come close to death on many occasions.

When I am still and quiet and listen closely, I can hear the voice of Jesus and God talk with me and answer my questions. The devil wants to get in the mix and get me to ignore what is being said to me. I have to fight the good fight to stay within the "stable" that God provides. I have to sit down and feel the grace, mercy, and love that are outpoured to me through the Holy Spirit. I don't have all the answers. In fact, I have few answers for I am a soldier trudging on the path of life. Some days are hard, but then God gives me reprieve so that hope pushes me further down the path to life and light. Take the time, don't give into the world's demands, and spend each and every day with your Lord. Trust me, it will make a difference in your life, your attitude, and your belief.

9

For the Beauty

SUNDAY, AUGUST 26, 2018

For the beauty of the earth, for
the beauty of the skies.[2]

What a wonderful morning to sit on the porch and hear the birds begin to sing their praises to our Creator, God. The morning is still more dark than light, but the world is becoming alive with sounds of nature—a true blessing from God for me this morning.

Much has happened this past week, but the main event is that my husband had a run-in with a table saw, and the saw won. The fact that he has been on a blood thinner for his clotting disorder and a couple of pills taken for his heart did not help. He bled from the cut on his thumb for four hours before the bleeding was stopped. One wouldn't think that someone could bleed that long with a thumb cut. Now, he will have surgery this week as he cut into the bone. Part of the bone is gone, the joint is dislocated, and he has a possible tendon tear. I was two hours away when all this occurred, but God looked after him. Our neighbor took him to the emergency

---

[2] Folliott S. Pierpoint and William Chatterton Dix, "For the Beauty of the Earth," 1864

room. He could have lost his thumb, hand, or even worse, but God took care of him. He told me that as he was working to complete the basement construction, and he heard an inner voice that said, "Don't mess with the sofa. Don't mess with the sofa." However, he ignored the inner voice and the cut occurred because he messed with the sofa. He knew that the way in which he was cutting a new leg for the sofa was unsafe, but he did it anyway.

God gives us choices in this life. Even when my husband heard the inner voice saying, "Don't mess with the sofa" and proceeded anyway, God still took care of him. So many times, we learn lessons the hard way. Our stubbornness, our desire to do it our way, and our human nature get in the way of our hearing the direction by the Holy Spirit. You might ask, "If God loved your husband, why did he get cut?" Because God loves us, he gives us choices. He doesn't dictate to us that we have to do something or not. He provided guidance to my husband prior to the accident; however, my husband, in his stubbornness, chose to ignore the warning. I have recently discovered that my mind has to be quiet in order for me to "hear" God within my soul. Our mental "busyness" is what keeps us from hearing God's directions. Even my typing of this note can keep me from hearing the voice of God through the Holy Spirit.

Jesus Christ, in His death and resurrection through the love of the Father for all His children, allows us to come into communion with God through the Holy Spirit. Even though I knew that my husband had cut his hand, I had a sense of peace as I drove for two hours to get to his side. I knew in my heart that everything was going to be OK. The Spirit comforted me as I drove the distance. There was no fear, and as such, the evil one could not overcome.

Each of us has struggles each and every day. Life has often been compared to a roller coaster, mountains and valleys, and waves in the ocean. Life is very much like these things. God created us to commune with Him. He created us to ask Him the questions, like a child asks a parent.

How do you find the peace, reassurance, comfort, and communion with God? The answer is simple. Just pick up the Bible and begin to read. Each time the book is opened, the Spirit reveals more than the last time. Ask for knowledge and understanding through the Spirit. Listen to the quiet voice of God. Ask for protection from Jesus Christ as you travel the roads of life. Trust that God will protect and provide for you as one of His little children. Ask for God's direction in everything you say and do throughout your day. Ask for His guidance in all your transactions.

I am so thankful that God never revealed the disappointments and illnesses that I would endure as I grew through the years. I probably would not have survived emotionally, mentally, and probably physically. In our growth, God makes us stronger. Reach out to Jesus; He connects us to our Creator. May the Lord bless you and yours today, tomorrow, and always.

10

Funerals

MONDAY, AUGUST 6, 2018

... but a woman who fears the Lord will be
greatly praised. Reward her for all she has done.
Let her deeds publicly declare her praise.
—Proverbs 31:31 (NLT)

This scripture was read at the funeral for my mother-in-law yesterday. My husband has always said that you can tell how someone impacted the lives of others at the funeral. The church was full even though the majority of his mother's friends had died before her. Her body was in the church, but her soul and spirit were gone. Funerals are not for the dead, but for the living. Funerals are for those who are "left behind." Tears were shed, but smiles of happiness appeared on many faces for we knew that she was absent in the body but alive in Christ. She had a very long life. I only knew her for a short period of time; I have been in the family for fewer than twenty years. I am so glad that I was able to visit with her briefly a week ago last Saturday. She seemed very alert to me at the time. I always loved to hear her stories. She was quite a character. I developed a relationship with her that was different from that I had with my mother. Even though she may have told the same stories over and over again, I never tired of hearing them. I only knew her in her later years. As I sit and type this, I remember a time about ten years ago when I came home from work and found her mopping my front porch. I wasn't expecting this from an eighty-year-old woman. She also helped decorate the Christmas tree the weekend that our renovated plantation-style house was on the Christmas Tour of Homes. She was as proud as we were of the renovations done to the old house that she had once played in as a young child.

Her body may be in the grave in the church cemetery; however, her soul is with the Lord. We can go to the cemetery and remember all the good times, but we can also remember those good times in our hearts and minds. She had a joyous reunion with her son, husbands, father, mother, grandparents, and many more. It is beyond our comprehension for we are human and can never really understand the workings of God. God places us where He needs us at the time. We need to listen to Him through the Son and the Spirit. The best type of work we can do on this earth is the work of the Lord.

May God continue to bless all of us. I am so thankful that He sent His Son, Jesus, to allow me to come into His presence in the future and to lead me today.

11

Gangs

Your love for one another will prove to
the world that you are my disciples.
—John 13:35 (NLT)

Once again, as I have written so many times before, I am amazed how God knows that the timing is just right for what I read in the Bible or a devotional book. David Jeremiah,[3] in the monthly devotional book that he wrote for September 2018, was right here for me today. He asserts that God knew us before we were created in our mothers' wombs. I too, have begun to realize this in the past year. If we read about it in the Bible with David's psalm, why would we not believe it? If we can see the image of a fetus inside the mother's womb months before the baby is born by an ultrasound (soundwaves producing the image), why do we not think that God knew us before He created us? With that being said, if we were with God before we were born, why would we not trust Him to provide for us now?

David Jeremiah compares the importance of timing in cooking to the creation of each and every one of us, helping us realize, as

---

[3] David Jeremiah, *Turning Points Magazine & Devotional*, September 2018.

he says, "that we aren't half-baked." God creates each of us in His image and after His likeness and places within our hearts His love for us. It is we who choose to ignore it or not accept it. If we accept it, He will be able to guide us in the way and the purpose of the life for which we have been created. Yes, I think God created each of us to be unique and different for a specific purpose, so that our lives might touch the lives of the person next to us. Even in a gang, isn't there always a leader? Don't the other members look up to the leader? What makes that leader different? What would happen if that leader could be changed through the love of Christ? Why did that person become a member of a gang? Was it because members didn't feel a sense of belonging prior to joining the gang? Were they promised an easy way to make a living?

One doesn't have to look at an actual gang situation to see the "gang" in any setting. Even when I attend a work conference, I see the same type of gang activity. I see people clamoring to be part of a specific group. How can we experience or give love to others if we are unwilling to move away from the gang and be different? Why are we scared to venture out? Even though we may be classified as adults, are we really? Are we not children of parents? Does our status as children ever change in the eyes of our parents? Are we all not children of God? Parents protect their children; a mother protects her children, like a bear protects her cubs. So if that is the case, why would we ever think that God, Christ, and the Holy Spirit wouldn't protect us? Could it be that we haven't opened our hearts to accept and feel the love of the Trinity?

Have you ever walked into a room and sensed that something was different about the people in it? You may not be able to put your finger on it if what you sense is a spirit of love, but you can definitely feel it if there is a sense of hate, unrest, or uncertainty. Is it possible that the room you walked into may have the presence of Jesus? Jesus taught us to have love and compassion for others just as we love ourselves. How can we love others if we haven't learned to love ourselves? Love is what can bring people together, while hate can cause people to quickly move away. Love is good and hate is evil. If we continue to focus on love and push evil thoughts away, we will find peace with one another in Christ.

These are thoughts to ponder, to think about, and maybe even trigger you to pick up the Word of God and seek, ask, and knock at the door so that the Spirit will lead the way in your life.

12

Gossip

WEDNESDAY, JULY 25, 2018

Let everything you say be good and
helpful, so that your words will be an
encouragement to those who hear them.
—Ephesians 4:29

I picked up a devotional from Charles Stanley[4] to read. I realized that I had read it before as I had written notes on the page. I carry Stanley's and Jeremiah's monthly devotional magazines with me as I travel for my job because I like to read, study, and ponder the scriptures first thing in the morning with my first cup of coffee; if I don't have much time, I read the devotional for the day. Stanley's title for his devotion today was "Our Anchor in Stormy Times." The questions that Stanley asked in this devotional were, "Where do these storms come from?" "Why does the Lord allow storms in our life?" and "How do we respond to storms?" Interestingly enough, these are the thoughts that I wrote down.

I picked this devotional today because one of my coworkers told me that another coworker had

---

[4] Charles Stanley, "Our Anchor in Stormy Times," *In Touch*, July 25, 2018.

about reading a passage in Ecclesiastes. My first thought was to read, "There is a time to be born, and a time to die" (Ecclesiastes 3:1 NLT); however, the Spirit led me to the verse written above. My mother-in-law is no longer struggling to breathe, no longer struggling to hear and to see clearly, no longer struggling to stand upright without falling, no longer struggling to live. She is absent in the body but present with the Lord. I thought about all this as I stood by myself over her body—so broken down and irreparable— yet I smiled because I knew that she was celebrating in God's house with family and friends.

My father is ninety years of age, and my mother will turn ninety in the next few days. God blesses those with long lives who have been faithful to Him. My parents are facing their struggles with aging bodies that might not be able to be repaired. They are struggling with the changes in their lives because they used to be independent and free. I know too that their struggles may be over soon.

None of us know the day or the hour when our toes will be turned upright in the grave. As I travel to perform work duties, I pass many cemeteries in small and large towns. As I glance at the headstones, I see big monuments and small ones. The one thing that all have in common is that everyone is on the same level. One grave is not better than another because all that were buried are dead. As we age, we ponder our own deaths. There is nothing wrong with that as God prepares us to enter His house through His Son Jesus Christ. The one important factor is that we believe in Christ and accept Him as our Lord and Savior. That is the only way that we can enter into our heavenly Father's mansion with many rooms. Christ prepares each of us a room; He prepared one for my mother-in-law—a special room, just for her.

14

Happiness

MAY 17, 2015

Wait on the Lord; Be of good courage.
And He shall strengthen your heart;
Wait, I say, on the Lord.
—Psalm 27:14 (NKJV)

Do you ever feel depressed, down, discouraged, or dead in life? Do you ever feel that life is overwhelming you and no one understands? Do you ever just want to run away because you feel that you will be happier elsewhere? Do you ever wonder if you will ever again be as happy as you were as a child? Do you ever wonder why you can't make something happen? Do you ever feel frustrated about your situation and you don't feel, want, or know how to climb out of your hole? Do you ever complain and then don't understand why others don't want to listen, don't know what to say, or don't understand? Do you ever feel that life isn't what you thought that it should be or how you want it to be? Do you ever wonder what you are supposed to be doing in your life? Do you ever wonder if there is a creator or higher spirit who loves you? Do you think that all the "God stuff" is stupid, old-fashioned, or nonexistent?

All I know is that God Almighty exists, He loved me as a

little child, and He still loves me as an adult child. He is the one who created me and made me unique as I was being formed in my mother's womb. I have tried to go my own way, and I have been a complete failure. I have been unhappy; I have often wondered where I am to go in life. I have wondered why I haven't gone on the path that I thought that I should.

We must go on the paths that He has chosen for us to find happiness; otherwise, life overwhelms us, discourages us, and depresses us. We must wait and listen for His direction. Jesus said, "Let the little children come to me" (Mark 10:14 NIV). Since we are children, He bids us to come to Him to find rest and happiness.

15

Heavenly Realm and Reality

MONDAY, DECEMBER 2, 2019

> God sits above the circle of the earth. The
> people below seem like grasshoppers to
> him! He spreads out the heavens like a
> curtain and makes his tent from them.
> —Isaiah 40:22 (NLT)

Isaiah wrote this passage of scripture long before people knew that the earth was round. How could he know that except that the Spirit whispered it in his ear? He continues to give us a clear understanding that God is so great that when God looks down from heaven, He sees us as grasshoppers. When in an airplane flying high in the sky, how do the earth and people below look to us? His hands spread out the heavens "like a curtain." Can you begin to imagine? How much more can this be described?

Just as the Spirit whispered into the ear of Isaiah, the Spirit can whisper in our ears. God gives us the choice whether to listen or not. If God did this for Isaiah seven hundred years before the birth of Christ, why can't He do it for us today? He can, and He will if only we follow His direction. How can I be so sure? For I know my personal Savior and friend. I know my Master. I know how the Spirit can work from within.

I witnessed that last night as my husband and I visited my elderly parents. I saw the Spirit speak through my father as he confessed his faith and belief. I saw the certainty within his being, which I had not seen in a long time. I saw the strength as he began to talk with my husband about faith, grace, and salvation. I saw the inner strength of a man who is ninety-one years of age yet not crippled in mind, even though his body is fading away. The Spirit gives us that type of strength through knowing and loving our Lord Jesus Christ.

Life's experiences teach us so much. We can decide to follow either the road to destruction or the road to life eternal. We think that we know so much in our youth, but unfortunately, we don't. Some are not exposed to the truth while growing up; some of us are, and it makes a difference as we struggle through life. I am in a struggle with life again, but I have the faith and assurance that God will carry me through as He has time and time again.

As we began the new liturgical year in churches with the beginning of Advent, let's remember the One who makes it possible for us to be clean and pure and allows us to come into the presence of God. Let's not forget, though, that God loved us so much that He sent His Son to be born, live an earthly life, and accept the responsibility to shoulder our sins on His body and eventually give up His life so that we could live forever with our Creator. Can you imagine that day? Can you dream of it as children dream of their futures?

So many times, I have caught my little granddaughter just staring out into space. I wonder if she sees her guardian angel and is watching what her angel is doing. Did you stare into space as child? Do you remember what you were thinking or seeing? I think that the heavenly realm is closer than we can see with these human eyes and that God gives us glimpses into that reality from time to time. We just can't ignore it but accept it for what it is. Do things happen by coincidence, as we would like to say, or is it God giving us that glimpse into the heavenly realm? Think about it as we approach the manger of the Christ child today, tomorrow, and always.

16

Impossible or Possible

THURSDAY, JANUARY 23, 2020

> Then Jesus said to his disciples, "I tell you the
> truth, it is very hard for a rich person to enter the
> Kingdom of Heaven.... Humanly speaking, it is
> impossible. But with God everything is possible."
> —Matthew 23:23, 26 (NLT)

When Jesus spoke these words to the twelve apostles, a rich young man had just finishing asking him the question about the deed that he had to do to gain eternal life. First, notice the word *deed*. Inheriting the blessing of eternal life deals with our inner being and our inner desire to have eternal life. We have to focus on marching to Zion instead of living just for today. We have to focus on following in the direction that Jesus tells us to go by listening to the inner voice that feeds our heart with joy. Our deeds won't get us into heaven, but we can through the grace of God and believing in His Son, Jesus Christ. Jesus tells us, "I am the way, the truth, and the life. No one comes to the Father except through me" (John 14:6 NLT). If Moses couldn't look upon the face of God and was physically affected by being in His presence, what makes us think that we can come into the presence of God except through His Son?

The rich young man had achieved worldly possessions, so he walked away saddened when Jesus told him that he would need to sell all his possessions and give the money to the poor. This would allow the man to be suitable to enter the kingdom of heaven. The world wants us to cling to our possessions and our money, but the reality is that God has provided what we need. Instead of listening to God's voice through the Holy Spirit, we take an attitude not so unlike the toddler who says, "I want this. I want that." To take a young child through a toy store causes the child to go into sensory overload, as I like to say. The child immediately wants to gather everything in sight to take with them. Have you ever bought your child a toy one day and by the next day the child has lost interest in the toy? The child strived and longed for more possessions, but as some grandparents like to say, "Just give that child an empty box; they will enjoy it so much more." A child who has an empty box will start to create something out of what we think is nothing. What seemed impossible minutes before, when the child received the empty box, the child has made possible by creating a toy through the gift of creativity given through our heavenly Father.

Just when we think that we have everything in life going the way we think it needs to go, something is thrown into the mix and everything changes. The problem is that we are focusing on ourselves instead of on what God wants us to do. How many times are you reminded of the *we* when you hear of or see that possessions weren't able to take the place of a broken relationship in a family or there is illness? Possessions didn't help in that situation, did they? Giving up physical possessions is very difficult because the world wants us to cling to them. If we come into this world without anything, why do we think that we can take our things with us? If we use our things to help others in the ways that Jesus instructed, do we not think that we will be blessed in so many other ways? As my husband likes to say, "God provides for our needs, not our greed."

While listening to a Christian radio station yesterday, I heard a man speak on setting "faith-based" goals for our lives. I had never heard of setting goals in that manner. He then went on to say that once we set these goals, we should meditate and even journal to see if this is what God wants us to do. This way, the focus is not on the goal of things but on how to touch others' lives while receiving blessings from God in our own lives. As I focus on preparing my house for weekend guests, I will do my utmost to prepare it so that the warmth of God is revealed through the beauty of the home. In return, we are blessed with receiving the money that it brings for those nights.

We attempted to sell this house for seven months without success. We then reevaluated the situation and realized that it would be better to rent this home on a yearly basis. We thought that God had sent a renter to us within days of this decision, but the possible renters backed out because, we were told, they had "too much furniture" for this home. Yes, we were disappointed; however, I trust that God will send another renter to us. We don't know what God has planned for us. We must wait patiently. God blesses us so that we can in turn bless others. May God bless you and yours today, tomorrow, and always.

17

In the Twinkling of an Eye

SUNDAY, SEPTEMBER 23, 2018

It will happen in a moment, in the blink
of an eye, when the last trumpet is blown.
For when the trumpet sounds, those who
have died will be raised to live forever.
And we who are living will also be transformed.
—1 Corinthians 15:52 (NLT)

"In the blink of an eye" came to my mind this morning as I sat in my rocking chair on the front porch of my home. It was sunrise, and the mist of the lake hid the mountains in the distance. The colors of the sunrise were magnificent, with light blue, orange, and pink. I looked down for less than a second and looked up again to find that the pink in the sky was gone. The sky was transformed.

One has to wonder: if the pink in the sky was gone in less than a second, why do we think that it is impossible for our earthly bodies to be transformed in order to enter the heavenly realm? If we focus on heavenly things instead of earthly things, is it possible that the Spirit will lead us to understand more clearly? We are plainly told in the Bible that "Adam, the first man, was made from the dust of the earth, while Christ, the second man, came from heaven."

If our bodies can be transformed into ones that can enter the heavenly realm, then we must believe, trust, and work enthusiastically for the Lord. "Nothing you do for the Lord is ever useless" (1 Corinthians 15:58 NLT). Just as I sit on my front porch looking at the mountains, listening to the sounds of nature and man, I sense a "peace of God which passeth all understanding" (Philippians 4:7 KJV). Jesus brings peace to our lives only if we listen to His whispering in our heart.

Lord, help me to become still and quiet in my mind and in my deeds so that I take the time to commune with you each and every day. Amen.

18

In My House Are Many Rooms

THURSDAY, OCTOBER 18, 2018

> There is more than enough room in my Father's
> home. If this were not so, would I have told you
> that I am going to prepare a place for you?
> —John 14:2 (NLT)

This morning as I lay in bed before the sun rose, I thought of this verse for some reason. I don't understand how the Spirit puts the verses in my mind at a specific time. It reminds me of a dream that I had several years ago about a big house with no staircase to the second floor and how the rooms seemed to extend beyond my ability to see from the first floor. I didn't and still don't understand why the second floor didn't have a staircase. I do know that the house was massive. Is God's home not going to be massive? Wouldn't you like a room where you will once again feel protected and your needs will be provided? Some, unfortunately, did not experience the joy that I had as a small child with loving, Christian parents. Even in a Christian home, there are difficulties, arguments, unrest, and at times a sense of impending doom; however, the love of Christ overshadows and resolves all. We are human beings with human characteristics that are far from perfection. We sometimes would like to think that we are perfect, but perfection will only be reached in eternity through the grace and love of our Lord Jesus Christ.

The darkness turned into day this morning with the most beautiful sky mirroring the reflection of the sun with different shades of orange and red. Clouds hang over some of the mountaintops in the distance as I look out my sunroom window; however, the sun shines brightly, showing the peace and love of our heavenly Father. It is a new day of opportunity to tell others about His love and grace, a most beautiful morning.

19

Lessons

SATURDAY, DECEMBER 28, 2019

> People do not live by bread alone, but by
> every word that comes from the mouth of
> God.—*Jesus*, in Matthew 4:4 (NLT)

I thought of this scripture this morning because my sister recently told me that my ninety-one-year-old mother wants to read and study her Bible for hours, even reading it instead of eating her breakfast. My sister is concerned that she needs food to sustain her, but I think otherwise. Food certainly is important, for that's how God created us; however, even when Jesus went without food in the wilderness and was tempted by the devil, He spoke the truth. There are two types of food—worldly food and spiritual food. Spiritual food trumps worldly food for me every time. Lessons for each of us can be learned at any age from others of any age.

I certainly understand why my mother takes a long time to read and study her Bible. I understand her desire to sit and read. I also understand that she may not be physically hungry due to her advanced age and that her body doesn't require much intake of worldly food. Just as a toddler will not eat lots of food each day or at each setting, an elderly person reverts to the same way of eating.

The body is slowing down as it continues to age and deteriorate. In fact, the body begins to age when a child is born. My mother has found the need to spend more time with her Lord, and that's OK. I certainly will not tell her otherwise. My sister has come to realize this too, as she schedules doctor appointments toward the end of the day instead of at the beginning.

I am sure that my mother is also making notes about her readings in a handwritten format, as she doesn't really know how to use a laptop. She at least tried to learn how to use one but eventually gave it up because of her aging. I may or may not have gotten my passion for writing from my mother. I suspect that it was passed down from my grandmother, as I have found her writings in old books. My grandmother tended to write poetry, which my older brother also enjoys writing. It certainly is amazing to me how these gifts and talents are passed down through the DNA from one generation to another.

As I prepare for yet another celebration of Christmas, I too take the time to sit and search, find, and write about those things that have inspired me through the Spirit. May the Lord bless you and yours today, and may you also inspire others through the gift of the Holy Spirit.

20

Life

MAY 9, 2012

Keep your creator in mind while you are young!
In years to come, you will be burdened down with
troubles and say: "I don't enjoy life anymore."
—Ecclesiastes 12:1 (CEV)

Life does bring troubles that burden us down. As an adult, I often reflect on my youth, especially my childhood, because those were times with no worries. We don't seem to understand why people with dementia seem to live in the past. Are they reliving joyful times? It is amazing to see how a doll placed in an old woman's arms can calm her. Does it remind her of her newborn child? My mother-in-law, who is eighty-seven years old, perks up when her family is around. She seems to gain strength. Does it remind her of a happy time? My own elderly father longs to sit and talk when I come to visit.

This reminds us that life is not about making lots of money. Life is not about keeping up with the Joneses. Life is not about depending on others to tell us what to do. Life is about enjoying each day to its fullest. Life is about listening to God's animals, smelling the roses that God provides, enjoying the taste of food that God gives us from our gardens, feeling the warmth of God's sun on our skin, seeing

God's wonderful creation, loving those around us, and telling others the good news. Life involves realizing that we are not enslaved to a dark grave but have hope in eternal life with our Creator, Son, and the Holy Ghost.

I can't even imagine life without hope. God gives us encouragement each day if only we listen. The greatest legacy to each of you may not be financial wealth but wealth from the sharing of my experiences and hope in our Lord, Jesus Christ.

21

Like a Child

FRIDAY, AUGUST 17, 2018

> But Jesus said, "Let the children come to me.
> Don't stop them! For the kingdom of Heaven
> belongs to those who are like these children."
> —Matthew 19:13 (NLT)

I sit in the sunroom in my home watching my granddaughter as she swings back and forth in her swing. Her pacifier is in her mouth, and as she is being rocked by the swing, she hears and watches a baby cartoon show on the TV. The music from the nursery rhymes are soothing. It is my hope that, now that she has been fed and is clean, the rocking and the background of soothing music will lull her to sleep for a little while.

Children are so dependent on others to care for their every need. We all started as children. Jesus tells us that heaven belongs to those who are like children. I have watched my aging parents as they have gone from being totally independent to being dependent on others for personal hygiene tasks, not unlike children who are learning to perform such tasks for themselves. As bodies begin to deteriorate and break down, movement becomes more difficult than it used to be. The flexibility and strength of older bodies are not sufficient to allow us to pull our feet up to our mouths like children developing the coordination and strength to begin to crawl, walk, and then to run. Death begins with birth. We don't like to think about death; however, it comes many times as a relief from the pain, the lack of movement, the deteriorating of the mind, the financial stresses, the loneliness, the isolation, and much more. Death can be a relief from living.

I think it is wonderful that Jesus reminds us that we must become like children to enter the kingdom of heaven. That takes a burden off of us regarding staying independent. Sometimes, we need to accept life as it is. Jesus tells us that it is OK to become dependent at any age on our heavenly Father to provide for our every need. All we need to do is believe in God's purpose to save us for eternity through His Son, Jesus Christ. The Father, Son, and Holy Spirit are only a whisper, a thought, or a prayer away from us. Just as a child reaches out to be picked up, we can reach out to God and the Son to be picked up. We must get past our stubbornness and selfishness to reach and to accept through faith.

My granddaughter remains awake as I finish this; however, she is content to rock, listen, and trust that her grandmother is right by her side as she swings back and forth. She knows that she can just whimper and someone will come to attend to her every need. May the Lord Jesus bless each of us today as He blessed the little children so many years ago.

22

Like a Rock

SEPTEMBER 27, 2018

For you are a slave to whatever controls you.
—2 Peter 2:19 (NLT)

Who would ever think that a simple fisherman would have been able to deliver such a message about Jesus Christ? When we think about being a slave, we think of being controlled by another person, but people can also be controlled by a "thing," such as drugs, alcohol, lust, power, money, and yes, even food. We can be misled by others if we don't know the truth.

Earlier, Peter reminds the reader, "A day is like a thousand years to the Lord, and a thousand years is like a day" (2 Peter 3:8 NLT). Peter tells us that God wants to save all His children and waits patiently; however, a time is coming when the earth will be destroyed. Peter refers to the "throwing of angels into hell" (2 Peter 2:4 NLT); the great flood in Noah's time; and the destruction of Sodom and Gomorrah. Peter further tells us that everything will be destroyed, but we have no timeframe in which this will occur. Many may profess to know, but only God knows. Jesus doesn't even know the day nor the hour. It will happen "like a thief in the night" (1 Thessalonians 5:2 NLT).

When I was younger and asked my dad why he didn't sleep longer in the morning, he always responded that he didn't want the Lord to catch him sleeping. He said that there would be plenty of time to sleep in heaven. There is much work to be done on this earth working with people. Peter tells us that the way to be prepared is to "be on guard, then you will not be carried away by the errors of these wicked people and lose your own secure footing. Rather, you must grow in the grace and knowledge of our Lord and Savior Jesus Christ" (2 Peter 3:17–18 NLT).

One of the best ways for me to grow in the grace and knowledge of the Lord is to focus on heavenly thoughts, commune with God through Jesus Christ, and read and study the Bible. For I can only understand through what is revealed to me by the Holy Spirit. Even as I type this note for you, dear children, I realize that maybe these notes need to be shared with others. Many things can enslave us; however, the "truth will set you free" (Jesus). We, on the other hand, must seek and we will find, knock and the door will be opened, ask and it will be given to us. Was Jesus referring to earthly treasures when he said this? I don't think so. Rather, I feel that He was referring to heavenly treasures. Evil does not want us to know the truth. Evil wants to lock us in and make us slaves to the world. Jesus desires to set all children free.

May the Lord bless you and yours as you go forth from this day. May the Lord remove the film from our eyes so that we can see the truth.

23

Miracle

THURSDAY, FEBRUARY 6, 2020

Jesus replied, "What is impossible
with man is possible with God."
—Luke 18:27 (NIV)

I'm up in the wee hours of the early morning. All is quiet except for
the occasional sound of rainfall outside. This verse, which is written
and used frequently, appears in three gospels: Matthew, Mark, and
Luke. It is often said that, since Mark is the oldest gospel, Matthew
and Luke took scripture from Mark and used it in their gospels.
Could it be possible that, since Mark recorded his gospel first, he
remembered things that Matthew may have missed? Could it have
been that, when Luke heard about the situation in which Jesus spoke
these words, he searched until he could interview someone who was
there at the time? Again, it is written, "What is impossible with man
is possible with God."

As I awoke, I turned to pick up my glasses off my bedside
nightstand. I know for a fact that I left the TV on last night,
listening to a Christian meditation program that helps me get to
sleep sometimes at night. I also know for a fact that I left both TV
controls next to me in the bed and left my glasses on my face. My

phone was on the bedside table. This morning, I found not only my glasses on the bedside table but also both of the TV controllers. I thought, *That is strange*. I also know that today, according to the weather forecast, it is going to be an unstable situation with snow to follow in the mountains tomorrow and the following day. Those thoughts were on my mind as I went to bed. I needed reassurance through the Christian meditation program to assist me in attaining a sense of peace, warmth, and comfort. Just as my little dog fiercely shook off the water from her coat last night after being outside to tend to business, I needed to shake off the world and its problems before I slept.

Most would say that I moved the glasses and controllers to the bedside table without remembering. I say that is not the case, as I slept the same way another night when my husband wasn't here. Then, who would have removed the controllers and my glasses and placed them on the bedside table? My guardian angel, that is who. Impossible, you say. "But for twenty-one days the spirit prince of the kingdom of Persia blocked my way. Then Michael, one of the archangels, came to help me, and I left him there with the spirit prince of the kingdom of Persia" (Daniel 10:13 NLT). Most scholars believe that Daniel was referring to the angel Gabriel. Gabriel tells Daniel that he was being blocked from getting to him by a worldly spirit prince (demon). Now, does this seem impossible? Yes, some say, for the book of Daniel was written many centuries ago and doesn't apply to today. I challenge you to begin to read the Bible, which is the history of life, and see if you don't detect a repeat of history even centuries later. The Holy Spirit opens our eyes and reveals much in our mind's eyes. The Holy Spirit is a means by which to communicate with God through Jesus Christ.

So with regard to who placed my glasses and TV controllers on my nightstand, it was my guardian angel, of course. Does that scare me? No, for I know that I am protected and much is given to me. If much is given to me, then should I not give much to others? *Much* doesn't always refer to money, but there are other ways we can give to others: through our smiles, our kindness, our words, our actions, and much more. We hear of children talking with imaginary friends when they are young. Is it possible that they are talking with their guardian angels?

24

Mother's Day

MAY 11, 2012

> I tell you the truth, unless you change
> and become like little children,
> you will never enter the kingdom of heaven.
> —Matthew 18:3 (NLT)

As Mother's Day draws near, this verse reminds me of being a mother. A commercial on television recently showed a mother and daughter talking while preparing supper. The daughter is about four years of age, and the mother is pregnant. The mother encourages the daughter to talk with the baby, so the daughter whispers to the mother's enlarged stomach, "You will love Mama." Children say the funniest, most precious, and most matter-of-fact things at the most unexpected moments.

 Children are so trusting of adults. How many times do two adults swing a child between them, and the child giggles and says, "More! More!" I once thought that taking care of an infant was difficult until I learned that it is much more difficult to take care of a teenager. I had the experience of dealing with the behavior of a two-year-old while simultaneously dealing with the behavior of a thirteen-year-old. What was I thinking? I did learn that their behavior was very similar.

As children of God, we have to trust that our heavenly Father will take care of us as adults. We have to become humble. Because children are so trusting, no one should ever take advantage of a child. My love for children goes back to my days as a child when I cared for my baby doll. I would swing and sing at the top of my lungs, trying to touch heaven with my toes. It was a time of joy, peace, and fun.

As we watch our own parents and grandparents age, we once again see signs that remind us of behavior similar to that of a child. How many of us think about their fragile and frail state of physical being? How many of us begin to use the term *precious* to describe our parents and grandparents? There comes a time when even they require that we attend to their physical needs. We all begin life as infants and end it in an infant state of being. That's why it is important to understand why Christ told us that we must become like little children to enter the kingdom of heaven. This happens through trusting, once again.

God gives me moments during my meditation time now to glimpse a beautiful day as the sunlight streams through my windows, a time for me to become like a child in wonder of how God created the world around me. I can just imagine sitting on the steps and continuously asking questions, just like a child. May God's peace be with you and yours this Mother's Day weekend, and may you celebrate the fact that God is our Father and that He knows how little children touch our hearts.

25

My Favorite Time of the Morning

TUESDAY, DECEMBER 24, 2019

> For a child is born to us, a son is given to us. The
> government will rest on his shoulders. And he
> will be called: Wonderful, Counselor, Mighty
> God, Everlasting Father, Prince of Peace.
> —Isaiah 9:6 (NLT)

It's early morning, the time I usually awake. All is quiet except for the gentle snoring of my husband in the bedroom behind the wall in our basement apartment. This is my favorite time of the morning—before the household awakens and I spend time with my Lord. The room is dim except for a small lamp and the fireplace, with its faux fire burning; it is so pretty with the embers and the red, pink, orange, and blue colors. It reminds me of the song "Silent Night." I always was an early riser, even as a child. This setting, with its darkness, calmness, and the hearth ablaze, takes me back to an earlier time in my life, when I would sit by the Christmas tree in our family's living room as a child, look at the multicolored lights on the tree, and think about the birth of the baby Jesus and Santa.

I have always gotten excited before Christmas Day. Now, as an adult, I enjoy preparing for Christmas Day, thinking about how I might plan the day for Christmas Eve leading up to Christmas Day tomorrow. I am thinking that I will bring my young granddaughter down in this small basement apartment and wrap presents as she plays. I will ask her mother to prepare a late lunch since she is such a good cook. I would like for all those here to attend the Christmas Eve service at our small church, have a light supper, and maybe come to the basement to end the day with a time of hot chocolate and time of reflection.

As my husband begins to awaken, I am getting ready to close this out. The whole reason for this celebration is the fact that God provided a way for His people to come back into the fold. We, like sheep, tend to stray, and the Master has to come and retrieve us time and time again.

26

Now I Can See

SATURDAY, NOVEMBER 17, 2018

They asked, "Who healed you? What happened?"
—John 9:10 (NLT)

As I continue to heal through the power of the Lord Jesus Christ, I thought of this scripture during the night. At night, the area on my leg where my knee joint was removed and replaced seems to become quite stiff from lack of movement. I worked through the night to keep from taking pain medication as I was trying to determine whether I was having pain or just discomfort from the stiffness. I know that soon, in order to do my exercises to improve my movement in this leg, I will need to take some medication. I am beginning to feel a sense of pain in the joint. It was after one of my nightly trips to the bathroom that I had a little talk with Jesus. It is a time of complete quiet with no disturbances. I remembered that Jesus healed the blind man who had been that way since birth. He most certainly will heal my knee so that I can walk better than I did prior to surgery. My recovery reminds me of an infant beginning to learn to stand and walk. My walking after surgery was very limited; I thought that I couldn't do it. In reality, I was able to bear complete weight on my repaired leg. My little infant granddaughters don't even let that stand in their way as they begin to become independent and attempt to stand and walk. I watch closely as they manipulate and move their legs in the strangest ways to gain strength and increase their endurance. Soon, they will both be walking and running without any thought whatsoever that they couldn't do so earlier.

The surgeon had the skills to perform the procedure of getting rid of the old knee joint and placing a new metal one in its place, but Jesus touched the surgeon's hands and performed the miracle of healing. When I was a small child in elementary school, I broke my wrist by tripping over another student's legs while running to my specific spot in gym class. I continued to do my push-ups as instructed by my coach; however, the pain became so unbearable that I had to tell him. He splinted my wrist, called my parents, and sent me to the office. My father picked me up from school to take me to the doctor. It was only after I got into my father's car that I began to cry. My father knew without a doubt that I had broken my wrist, which was confirmed by the doctor through an x-ray.

My father told me at that time that the doctor could set the bone, but only Jesus could cause the healing to happen. I didn't understand at my young age the truth behind my father's statement, but now, I grasp it firmly in my heart. I have to be like my infant granddaughters and concentrate on moving my leg with exercise to strengthen my leg so that I can once again walk without much thought. I know, though, that Jesus is the one who will heal me. I go to Him in prayer and ask for strength to overcome the pain of the surgery and the exercise. Jesus doesn't tell me that I am not to take pain medication, for He knows that I need it to perform the exercises. What He does say to me is, "Rely on Me to help you; listen to Me so that I can help you." Last night, He told me to not do my exercises so late in the evening as it would increase my swelling and stiffness during the night. He told me to concentrate on the exercises in the morning and the early evening to allow the swelling to decrease by slowing down before bedtime. I am going to follow His instructions. Listen to Jesus. He is only a whisper away.

27

Open My Eyes

MONDAY, JANUARY 7, 2019

And let us not neglect our meeting
together, as some people do, but encourage
one another, especially now that the
day of his return is drawing near.
—Hebrews 10:25 (NLT)

"Open my eyes that I might see glimpses of truth thou hast for me."[5] This old hymn says it all. The truth is the truth, and the truth will set you free from the burdens of this old world. The truth will open your eyes to see past this old world and focus on the heavenly realm. As I sat and took the time to read several chapters in Hebrews, my eyes were opened again. So many times, I am like a child who has to be told something over and over again until I finally grasp the truth.

As all my children have returned to school or work after the Christmas celebration of 2018, and as I prepare to return to work in a month, I sit at my kitchen table, in the house by myself, with one candle burning as I come before God this morning. I am able

---

[5] Clara H. Scott, "Open My Eyes, That I May See," 1895.

to come to God through Jesus Christ, His Son, and Christ sends the Holy Spirit to guide and protect me. What a comfort. My eyes were opened this morning, and it seems that they are every time I read the scripture. That is why I want to write these notes—to share my experience of coming into the presence of our God. God is not just my God; He is your God too. Every time I read the scriptures, and even though I may have underlined a verse in a previous reading, I find another word that clarifies the meaning of the verse. This is why I have stated over and over again that the Bible is living.

I awoke last night from the beginnings of a bad dream and got up to make sure that no one had broken into the house, and all seemed well. It seems as if evil lurks at night. As a child might do, I reassured myself and went back to bed, but I prayed that God, Christ, and the Holy Spirit would provide protection for me throughout the night. My belief allowed me to sleep. As a little girl, my parents would have to leave the hall light on at night because of my fear of the shadows in my room. God always provided my guardian angel to watch over me and continues to do so.

My dear daughter, you told me that you and your husband saw a "ghost or spirit" floating above your daughter's bed as she slept yesterday morning, but you sensed peace. Christ doesn't want us to be afraid. He wants us to put our trust, love, and belief in Him. I suggested that this was probably your daughter's guardian angel. Could this be a way that Christ makes us realize that we need Him? I believe that angels and demons surround us all the time. The battle that exists is in the spiritual realm. The demons attempt to get us to do things that are not pleasing to God, and the angels fight to make us realize the truth through Jesus Christ. "Open my eyes that I might see glimpses of truth thou hast for me." When my eyes are open, I can see beyond this world. I can be transformed into the heavenly realm and visualize the unseen truth that Christ has for me. I can focus on the path and the journey to the heavenly gate. Is it possible that we have been in heaven before and just can't remember?

Is it possible that God sent us to this earth for a unique purpose? If this is possible, then why would we not want to return to heaven?

May the Lord bless you and keep you, and may His light shine upon you and yours and give you peace today, tomorrow, and always.

28

Our Rock

> He alone is my rock and my salvation, my
> fortress where I will never be shaken.
> —Psalms 62:2 (NLT)

I thought that I was up early enough that my husband would continue to sleep while I wrote and spent time with my Lord, but I just heard the closet door in the bedroom open, which tells me that he is ready to start his day. Sometimes, I just want the house to be extremely quiet as I spend time with my thoughts and with God. I think that we all need this time every day. It is easier to find the time than we think. We just have to make the time in our busy schedule. To hear noise in the house, though, is also a blessing, for it tells us that we aren't physically alone. Alone time can be nice, but it can also be a sad time for we feel as if we have no one. However, is that really the case?

I run to read from the book of Psalms in times of trouble. My heart feels the same way that David expressed his heart to God in times of delight and distress. I never thought that I could understand the meaning of the psalms, but God has enlightened me through the years. Maybe it was because I didn't take the time to understand by spending time with God each day. He kept a watch over me and continues to do so today. Even though my father is still on this earth at the age of ninety-one, even though I love my father dearly, and even though I have turned to him so many times in the past and still seek his advice, I have come to realize that in times of distress and joy, I turn and run to my heavenly Father. I know without a doubt that I was with Him before my time on this earth; I know that I was born with a unique skill and talent to show others the way; I know that He has protected and provided for me; I know that He put me to live on this earth at this very moment; I know that He allows me to make decisions and watches me even though I may make mistakes over and over again; and I know that He loves me "for the Bible tells me so."

As I struggle with life, I turn to my heavenly Father to help me find the time, remind me of the tasks at hand, and protect me from the evil that lurks around me and wants to distract me from what I have been instructed to do. I know that, if I put my faith and trust in my Lord, He will protect and provide for me.

Life is like riding in a boat on an ocean. Some days the ocean is rough and we encounter many waves, even to the point that we feel that our boats will capsize and we will surely drown. Other days, it is calm, and we can see for miles in all directions. Life is also like being among the mountains. Some days, the mountains seem too difficult to climb and we want to stay in the valley. Other days, the top of a mountain beckons us to come and view the scenery all around. Life can also be like a roller coaster. Some days, the ride is rough and curvy, but other days it seems like we are on a carousel as we feel the soft breeze blow in our faces. The world wants us to think that everything is like a bed of roses, but don't roses have thorns that can prick us as we reach to pick them?

I hope that you will turn to the One who can provide peace and comfort in your heart, mind, soul, spirit, and very being during your difficult and joyful times. I hope that you can imagine within your mind's eye that our heavenly Father has His arms wide open, waiting for us to run to Him to be comforted and to express our joy.

29

Passion

MONDAY, DECEMBER 3, 2019

> And it came to pass in those days that a
> decree went out from Caesar Augustus
> that all the world should be registered.
> —Luke 2:1 (NKJV)

As I am up early this morning before the break of dawn, I thought of this scripture as we begin the journey once again to the manger in which our Lord and Savior was born—a free gift from God, our Father, overseen by the Holy Spirit. The Spirit always tends to lead me where I need to go and where I need to look to encourage me along the way. I began to read the introductory summary written by David Jeremiah for Luke.[6] Jeremiah used several descriptive adjectives in writing about Luke, such as *compassionate, thoughtful, careful observer*, traits that we all hope our doctors would have in taking care of our physical needs. Something struck me, though: "Luke set aside his practice to pursue a venture that will absorb his time for years to come.… The great passion of Luke's life was writing

---

[6] David Jeremiah, *The Jeremiah Study Bible, NKJV* (Brentwood, TN): Worthy Books, 2013.

a two-volume history of the founding of Christianity." Jeremiah further writes, "The compassionate physician makes sure that the outcasts and the downtrodden of the world know they are invited to the banquet represented by the Kingdom of God." The training that I received throughout my schooling to be a nurse and my professional experience has taught me that we are never to give special treatment to the wealthy, but to treat each individual equally, no matter their color, religion, sex, race, or financial status.

I understand Luke's passion, for I too have developed a passion to tell others about our Father, the Son, and the Holy Spirit. It began quite innocently as a way for me to write my thoughts and feelings to help myself with my life's struggles; then, I began to focus on writing these notes to my children to maybe assist them in their life's struggles; and now, it has turned into a passion to share a little of my thoughts with others that might help them on their journeys. The evil one is still lurking nearby, trying his best to pull me away from this passion and distract me so that the task at hand will not be accomplished. I have pushed ahead by purchasing a package from a well-known publishing company to self-publish the first book; however, I am dragging my feet again. I figure it is Christmastime and I need to prepare. As I type this note, I think, *Am I going to be like the bridesmaids who didn't bring enough oil to ensure that their lamps kept burning while they awaited the arrival of the bridegroom?* (Matthew 25:1–13 NLT).

Lack of success, fear, anxiety, and much more knock at the door. God has helped me time and time again; all I have to do is say, "Here I go, Father. Take my hand and guide me through the door to this unknown area." Maybe, just maybe, the fear of the unknown ties into my recurring dream of the house with many rooms where I can't see what's in the rooms or see to the back of the house. As we prepare for the celebration of the coming of the Christ child, let us focus not on the world but on the manger in the lowly stable. May God bless you and yours during the Christmastide.

30

Peace

TUESDAY, NOVEMBER 20, 2018

> Does anyone want to live a life that is long
> and prosperous? Then keep your tongue
> from speaking evil and your lips from telling
> lies! Turn away from evil and do good.
> Search for peace and work to maintain it.
> —Psalm 34:12–14 (NLT)

Truth is found in the words written above so many centuries ago. Truth is the same today as yesterday and tomorrow. The tongue is one of the smallest members of the body, but it inflicts more pain than any other part. We must learn to control our tongues, or our tongues will control us. So many times, I am guilty of saying something before I really think about how it might affect another person. So many times, we don't realize how our tongues have impacted another person.

Is it just possible that, if we search for peace, our lips might not focus on lies and our tongues will not speak evil? What is peace? Is it different for you than for me? How does it make one feel if peace is in one's life? Is it possible to have peace? What makes it not possible to have peace? *Peace* is defined in the dictionary as "freedom from disturbance, quiet, and tranquility." What is tranquility? The quality or state of being calm.[7] Can you imagine how you would feel with complete calm? Can you imagine how the world would be with complete calm?

Many do not understand the guidance that we can get by reading the Bible; however, the Bible has provided guidance throughout the ages and the message has not changed. How can we find the guidance for living if we don't pick up the book where the truth lies within the pages? The book is free for all to open and explore. The more we explore and search for the truth, the more we find peace that is offered through our Lord Jesus Christ and the more we understand and ponder the truth within the pages. Jesus told us that the "truth will set you free." It will set us free from the burdens of sin. The truth revealed within the pages not only instruct but also express the love that God has for His human creation. If God created us in His image and His likeness, why would He not love us? Do not parents love their children? Do not parents care for their children? Why would we think any different about our heavenly Father?

If you don't pick up the book, then you will never find the truth. If we can pick up a book on the best-seller list, what is our reason for not picking up the Bible, which has been the best-selling book throughout the ages?

---

[7] Dictionary.com

31

Realization

TUESDAY, JULY 31, 2018

> The Lord is my Shepherd; I shall not want.
> He makes me to lie down in green pastures;
> He leads me beside the still waters,
> He restores my soul.
> —Psalm 23:1–3 (NKJV)

I have finally realized that if I intend to share this book with my children and possibly others, then I need to focus on typing the notes that were originally handwritten and put them in some semblance of order to send to a publisher. I started writing these notes as a way to ponder the scripture and how my life fits into God's path for me. I have always tended to follow what others wanted me to do or accomplish instead of focusing on where I know that I need to go. Never in my wildest dreams would I have thought that I would enjoy writing as I do. It seems so many times that my pen is not held by my hand but by the Spirit. In my later years of life, I realize that I have not really followed my God-given talent.

It is so easy to get so caught up in the everyday tasks of life that we forget to focus on our Creator and the blessings that He provides to us. It has taken me a long time to feel comfortable in my own skin and not worry about what the world thinks of me. Of course, I continue to struggle with that from time to time. I have always been the one who has provided the most financially for my family. That is a role that, for some reason, I felt that I needed to assume. Even as I am out on the road doing a job, I wonder, is this where I really want to be? I knew it was something that I could do, but I have come to realize that as we age, we need to focus on producing income instead of providing the manual labor of a task.

God blessed me and answered my prayers; however, now I am reevaluating what I asked God to give me. I have always felt that there is a purpose for God's leading us down certain paths. God wants to give to His children, but we are so stubborn that we decide that we want to go our own way instead. It is my hope and prayer that God will allow me to earn income in another way that meets His purpose instead of mine.

I will be taking a leap of faith, for I don't know where He might be leading me. How can I find out, though, unless I try? To get out of my comfort zone will create stress; however, Jesus will be nearby. We are reminded of that in Psalm 23:1–3a: "The Lord is my shepherd; I shall not want. He maketh me to lie down in green pastures: he leadeth me beside the still waters. He restoreth my soul" (KJV). It amazes me, how verses that I memorized as a child come back to me when I need them most. Each day I am learning more and more to "lean on the everlasting arms" of Jesus.[8] Lord, give me protection and knowledge to do the task at hand today. Be with my loved ones and keep them safe.

---

[8] Anthony J. Showalter & Elisha Hoffman, "Leaning on the Everlasting Arms," Tennessee Music and Printing, 1887.

32

Relationships

FRIDAY, DECEMBER 20, 2019

> So again I say, each man must love
> his wife as he loves himself, and the
> wife must respect her husband.
> —Ephesians 5:33 (NLT)

Nurturing relationships can be tough. Some days, weeks, months, or even years can be tougher than others, especially when it comes to marriage and family. It is not so difficult in the business world because our livelihoods are based on those relationships, and as a result, we tend to be more willing to nurture them. We do, however, tend to attack those we love the most for we know that, while they may not like it, they will accept it because we are family.

A family begins with the unity of two people and remains a family whether children are added to the equation or not. What better way for the devil to attack us than to attack a couple, which in turn trickles down to the rest of the family. This creates an opportunity for others, especially our children, to see how poorly we handle situations in times of stress through our lack of respect and love for our spouses.

Christmas is supposed to be a time of rest, calm, joy, anticipation, and especially love as we celebrate the birth of the Christ child. Unfortunately, the world wants us to focus on its values for Christmastime by agreeing to do things that we feel obligated to do; to spend beyond our means, which can create a financial burden in the future; and to enjoy the hectic and chaotic days that once were cherished within the immediate family as we took time out from our daily chores.

We must remember that the reason for this season is not Santa but the Christ child. It is a time to remember those things that we loved as children and to become "like a child" for the month of December. It means that, just as children strive to nurture their relationships with their parents by being good, we must really work hard to nurture the relationships that we have as a family. This nurturing must begin with the couple that started the family.

Christmas is a time for memories, but our focus should be on the Christ child in the manger. If we focused on the Christ child throughout this season and remembered what He did for each of us, would it not make us realize the importance of nurturing our relationships with our families? Let's not give up so easily on our relationships. Let's not go pout, grumble, or complain about our families. Let's enjoy each and every day that God has given us to be part of our families. Let's respect others more, let's love others more, and let's focus on giving of ourselves to others just as Christ gave Himself for us. May the light of Christ shine brightly for you and yours always.

33

Right Steps

SUNDAY, FEBRUARY 2, 2020

We can make our own plans, but the
Lord gives the right answer....
Commit your actions to the Lord,
and your plans will succeed....
We can make our plans, but the
Lord determines our steps....
The path of the virtuous leads away from
evil; whoever follows the path is safe....
Those who listen to instruction will prosper;
those who trust the Lord will be joyful....
We may throw the dice, but the
Lord determines how they fall.
—Proverbs 16:1, 3, 9, 17, 20, 33 (NLT)

Sometimes, in our anxiety, we can take a misstep and choose wrongly. If we allow God to show us the way, then we will be protected from harm and missteps. I have made many missteps on my path home because I wanted to do it my way.

God has blessed us with a tenant in our home. Everything seems fine, and we trust that He will protect our home as we work on the homestead that my husband's family built so many years ago. It is due for an upgrade, and we feel the need to be closer to family. This home won't be ours, but we will be able to use it. For all I know, God may know that this is the place in which I will be able to continue to write *Notes from Mama*, in a peaceful, country setting.

We can make the plans, but we better keep God in the forefront for He ultimately decides the outcome. We might throw the dice, but God determines how the dice fall. If we follow the path that God directs and instructs us to follow, then He will provide and protect us. We must go to God in prayer to ask for guidance from Him. He provides that protection and guidance through our communion with Him through the Holy Spirit.

He provided that protection and guidance to show us the way home through sending His only Son to be born of a virgin mother and live, breathe, and eventually die for our sake, which would allow us to come into His presence just as Adam and Eve once stood. This is not a fairy tale, it is not a myth, and it is not make-believe; it is real. It is as real as the time I walked with Jesus in my family's garden as a little girl. Many would say that it wasn't possible, but everything is possible with God. Everything is possible to those who believe.

As I continue to struggle with submitting my manuscript for publication due to distraction, I realize that I needed this time with my Lord and Savior, Jesus Christ. I need Him to help me cross over the stumps along the path. I am determined to get past the distractions and submit my writing for publication, and I trust that He will provide the right answers for me.

34

Struggles

TUESDAY, JANUARY 29, 2019

Remember, it is sin to know what you
ought to do and then not do it.
—James 4:17 (NLT)

It's hard to believe that we have begun another year, a year in which none of us knows what will really happen in our lives. I sit at the kitchen table and see the wetlands in front of my eyes. Earlier this morning, I heard two flocks of birds fleeing from the impending storm that will send snow to parts of the mountains. I sit alone thinking of the process of our move from this house to the mountain house. I have to admit, though, that my heart is not in returning to work in my long-held profession. It has always been my safeguard, but now, in my older age, it seems like more of a liability. Maybe God had to get me to this point in my life to make me move forward and follow His plan and the path that He has set before me, instead of me trying to decide what I think that I need to do.

I have kept journals for years. I turned to journaling as a way to express my thoughts. It was a way to express anger, disappointment, anxiety, frustration, and much more. In my journaling I have finally realized that this may be where God wants me to be. My writing will be Christian based whether it is fiction, nonfiction, or historical. My writings will always be based on Christian principles, for how else will others begin to know the truth for themselves?

My writings also began as a way to communicate my thoughts to each of you, my children; however, as I have continued, God has directed my desire to communicate the truth to others as well. Oh, how I struggle with this earthly mind instead of focusing on God's spirit that resides within my heart. The devil stands close by to thwart my natural calling in this life. Christ overcomes the devil if we request it. I am reminded that "humanly speaking, it is impossible. But not with God" (Mark 10:27 NLT). Everything is possible with God. I am further reminded to "think about the things of heaven, not the things of earth" (Colossians 3:2 NLT). My focus has to be on Christ, just as Peter was able to walk on the water while his focus was on Christ. When Peter lost his focus is when he began to slip into the water. Jesus reached out His hand and saved him.

Just as Jesus saved Peter from drowning, Christ has saved me physically, emotionally, mentally, and financially over and over again. Just when I thought that I was drowning, Christ reached out His hand and pulled me up from the grave. So many times, parents don't let children know of the struggles that they have experienced in their lives because they're always trying to protect their children. I have almost physically drowned twice, and I was within literal inches of being hit by a car on a dirt road at the age of five when my bike slid in front of a car. I have had to restart my life emotionally and financially twice. I have battled depression, anxiety, anger, and much more.

Through God's amazing grace, He has provided protection, peace, and love to me during these difficult times. Life on this earth isn't easy. Living on this earth means having ups and downs, bouncing in the waves in the ocean, and not knowing what to do. It's taken me a long time to find peace even though I was raised in a Christian home. We have no guarantees in this life. This is why it is so important to know and follow the truth—the truth found through Jesus Christ. May the Lord bless you and yours today, tomorrow, and always.

35

Thanksgiving

THANKSGIVING DAY, NOVEMBER 22, 2018

> May the Lord bless you and keep you. May
> the Lord make his face to shine upon you, and
> be gracious to you. May the Lord lift up his
> countenance upon you, and give you peace.
> —Numbers 6:24–26 (BSB)

As I continue to recover from surgery, I am up early. I had forgotten how much surgery will cause fatigue from just the simple tasks that were quickly accomplished prior to surgery. God teaches patience when our bodies don't perform as quickly as they once did. Learning patience has also allowed me to reflect on past events and times. To stay focused on the past is not healthy; however, we need to reflect from time to time as this can bring back wonderful memories. God plants these memories so that we are able to pull from them and share them with others, especially those we love.

Yesterday, as our grandson was visiting us during the holiday week, I pulled down the *Children's Bible Story Book* that my parents had given to my firstborn child for her first Christmas. That Christmas was tough for me as I was suffering from postpartum depression. The next Christmas, however, was a wonderful time as I had overcome the depression and was enjoying my child to the fullest.

As I flipped through the pages of that book, I came upon pieces of paper where I had written down various information. I found a fax that had been sent to me at my employer's office seventeen years earlier. My mother had sent an advent program from her workplace. I also found where I had written down the assignment for the children in the Sunday school class that I taught about their specific roles in lighting and explaining the advent wreath at church. I had long forgotten the name of the little boy who developed a friendship with my son during that year of emotional strife until I saw his name on the piece of paper that I discovered this morning. And this brought back other memories of me teaching a Sunday school class with just this child and my child. I remember well, though, the love of the small church congregation that encircled my son and me as we attended every Sunday morning. I remember that my son and I would often go eat out with church members after church service. I remember how the congregation seemed to grow after my son and I began to attend. I remember that the church members were sad to see us leave after I made the decision to move back to my home state so that my children could be close to my parents and siblings after separating from my husband.

As I continued to flip through the pages of the Bible storybook, I discovered a small photograph of my second child and myself. I don't know who decided to take that photograph and cut just her and me out to be separated from the remainder of the picture. I suspect that it may have been the daughter in the picture, but could it have been my son? He used to like to cut paper into small shreds when he was bored. This photograph was taken during Easter, when my daughter was probably eighteen months of age. She was standing but I was holding her more upright. Both of us were dressed in our new Easter dresses. She now has a child who is almost a year of age. I will take a picture of this small photograph and send to her this morning as a reminder.

I shared other memories with my grandson yesterday, as he helped me unwrap the pieces of the nativity set to arrange on the living room table for all to see. I have pieces from three different nativity sets, as pieces have been broken throughout the years. I began with a set when my first child was small, the second set was bought at a retail store, and the last set was brought at an estate sale. Even though the pieces were placed carefully and lovingly upon the table, an ear broke off of the cow's head. When I viewed the damage, I saw that I had reglued the ear in the past—a reminder that accidental breaks occur with little hands. I will try to locate the glue gun and reattach the ear once more. I did ask my grandson to tell me the story of the first Christmas. He did quite well with the story except for the time frame of the visit from the wise men.

We all can bring memories to the table this Thanksgiving Day and thank our Lord and Master for His blessings upon us. New memories can be created and others shared. My son's girlfriend shared her family's memory of a special Greek dish that her grandmother made every Thanksgiving. She spent a lot of time last night making this dish for all to share and enjoy this Thanksgiving Day. Our purpose is to share the love of our Lord Jesus Christ toward others and to assist them on their journeys just as others have assisted us. May the Lord bless you and keep you today, tomorrow, and always.

36

The Lord Is My Shepherd

TUESDAY, OCTOBER 9, 2018

> But you have received the Holy Spirit, and
> he lives within you, so you don't need anyone
> to teach you what is true. For the Spirit
> teaches you everything you need to know,
> and what he teaches is true—it is not a lie.
> —1 John 2:27 (NLT)

If the Spirit lives within us, then we will know the truth. What we have to do is be quiet and listen to the voice of the Spirit from within our being. It makes sense, for we are created in the image and likeness of God. God gives us a choice whether to believe or not. The devil would like to lead us astray. The devil doesn't want us to see the light but to continue to live in the darkness of the world. The devil may be the ruler of the world, but God, Christ, and the Holy Spirit continue to reign over the devil, the devil's followers, and the world. That may be why Paul taught us to not conform to the world but to be transformed by the renewing of our mind. The mind can be easily swayed at any phase in our lives.

If God is for us, who can be against us? Last week I traveled to my office, which is located in the downtown area of a large city. I have to stay in a hotel when working there because of the driving distance from my home. I walked every morning and afternoon, most days by myself. I felt as if I had an angel in front of and an angel behind me for protection. I was never approached by anyone who would harm me. I really didn't see the purpose of my going for the specific training that I was going to receive, but then I realized after several days in training that God had sent me there for the experience of being with others who proclaim His name. I was surrounded by others who possess the light. It made me bold too. It made me realize the value of community with other followers of Christ. There is strength in numbers as well.

Even as I listen to the weather report as a hurricane bears down on a neighboring state that will affect our state, instead of feeling fear, I have a feeling of peace and calm. The devil will destroy the peace and calm if our minds allow it. But all things are possible in Christ who strengthens us, the Spirit of the One who lets us know the truth that is within our very being. I just have to take the time and listen. Not only do I have to listen, but I have to follow where the Spirit leads me.

37

The Man and the Mat

SUNDAY, NOVEMBER 11, 2018 (VETERANS DAY)

> They couldn't bring him to Jesus because of
> the crowd, so they dug a hole through the roof
> above his head. Then they lowered the man
> on his mat, right down in front of Jesus....
> "Stand up, pick up your mat, and go home!"
> —Mark 2:4, 11 (NLT)

Before I went to bed last night, I asked Jesus to let me sleep throughout the night without waking up to take pain medicine for the knee replacement surgery I had a couple of weeks ago. I have had to control my pain by developing a routine of taking pain medication to allow me to perform my knee exercises and to prevent spikes of pain, which I experienced a few days after the surgery. I am now in the process of decreasing this pain medication so I don't develop a dependency on it. This has been a very difficult surgery and quite unexpected. I have had lots of swelling in my leg, which limits my ability to flex my knee. Removal of the staples was quite painful because the swelling had made the staples dig into my skin. I could tolerate the removal of only two staples at a time, which produced bleeding and pain. I tolerated this procedure for the removal of at least twenty staples. The pain medication that was in my system did not help with the pain.

During the night, I awoke on several occasions to stretch my leg. The swelling of the limb has the sensation of a forty-pound weight pulling on my leg. The swelling is worse in the evening and night. I continue to perform my leg exercises but made a decision to rest more and ambulate less yesterday but to perform some household tasks that I have not done in the past couple of weeks. When I awoke, I felt the pressure of the swelling, but the pain was not unbearable. Each time I awoke during the night, I thought of the parable of the paralyzed man on a mat. He was lowered down through a hole dug by his friends from the rooftop because of the crowd surrounding Jesus. This man must have been admired by his friends because it took at least four people to lower him from the roof so that he would be in front of Jesus. As I lay in bed, I remembered how Jesus told the man to get up, pick up his mat, walk, and go home. I thought that if Jesus did that for this man, He could help me through the night. So many times, it is me that limits Jesus's ability to heal or help me because of my negative mindset. The unseen evil forces that surround me put doubt in my mind. If I turn loose, be still, and listen to the voice of Jesus, He tells me that He is with me, hears me, and knows my needs before they are a thought in my mind.

I sang praises to Jesus this morning, and He added the icing on the cake when I looked out my sunroom window and saw the beginning of day with a distant star and the sunrise reaching the tops of the mountain range. It was a true beauty to behold. Praise be to God the Father, Jesus the Son, and the Holy Spirit. It is a beautiful day to remember those men and women who died for us so that we may be free. Freedom in Christ is wonderful.

38

The Power of God

FRIDAY, NOVEMBER 30, 2018

> Mary asked the angel, "But how can
> this happen? I am a virgin."
> —Luke 1:34 (NLT)

As I watched the movie *The Star*, which came out in the theaters last year, I was watching to see how closely the story would parallel the scriptural account in the Bible. Liberties were taken, but the movie seemed age appropriate and had a sweet message in the fact that Bo may have represented the littlest angel or the little drummer boy. It also explains why I needed to correct my own grandson on the sequence of events. But at least it encouraged him to tell me the real purpose for celebrating the season and the Christmas story as he helped to place the nativity set on the table in the foyer of my home.

I was quite happy to see that this film was not the traditional Christmas movie that has appeared in theaters in the past. It encouraged little ones to ask questions, especially if they had never been introduced to the real story of Christmas. The gifts from the wise men for the baby Jesus helped to explain why we give and receive presents at Christmas. As a child of ministers, I was never denied gift giving and receiving. I knew the Christmas story and played the role of Mary many times as a child. Our focus was on Jesus, but my parents also allowed us to believe in Santa Claus. They allowed me to make choices even as God allows us to make choices. My parents had rules, but doesn't God also have rules?

As the time to celebrate Jesus's birthday arrives, let us remember the real reason for the season. Let this be a time of fun, celebration, love, blessings, and thankfulness that God loved us so much that He sent His only Son to die for our sins. We have three in one—God the Father, God the Son, and God the Holy Spirit with us now, tomorrow, and forever.

39

The Power of Prayer

FRIDAY, AUGUST 31, 2018

Now I have an answer for my enemies;
I rejoice because you rescued me.
—1 Samuel 2:1 (NLT)

The birth of Samuel was like the birth of Isaac. Hannah and Sarah were born barren, and both were ridiculed—Hannah by her husband's other wife, and Sarah by her handmaid who had conceived a child through Abraham. Hannah gave her son, Samuel, to the service of God from the time that the boy was weaned. She freely gave him to be raised in the tabernacle in Shiloh. This had to be very difficult; however, she kept her promise to God. God blessed Hannah with three more sons and two daughters after Samuel. I found this verse this morning as I searched in the concordance for scripture on the power of prayer. In my humanity, I forget so easily the "power of prayer."

The best defense against Satan is also the best offense, the power of prayer. I have known about prayer since I was a little girl; however, I didn't put much thought into the fact that prayer allows us to defend ourselves against the evil nature of the world. It is the humanity and the sin that crept into the world that caused the evil. This was evident as I continued to read the scripture about the wickedness of Eli's sons, who were priests from the tribe of Levi. Because Eli didn't discipline his sons, God told him, "All the members of your family will die before their time. None will reach old age" (1 Samuel 2:31 NLT). Even though Samuel was raised in the temple of God from a child, he too suffered with sons who were wicked. Was that the result of watching the relationship of Eli with his sons? It seems that, many times, we follow in the ways that our parents interacted with us as children as we raise our own children.

Prayer is what protects us, shields us, and keeps us safe. We may not like the answer that God gives to our prayers, but there is a reason. If we don't pray, how will we be protected, shielded, or kept safe in this world? It seems that I have finally come to the realization that prayer needs to be continuous. It doesn't need to occur just at mealtime or bedtime but all the time. Lack of prayer leads to an inability to address issues in a sensible and calm way. Prayer allows us to use our minds and emotions to talk it out with God and lay it all on the table through our Lord, Jesus Christ. Jesus gives us the ability to commune with God through the Holy Spirit. He is a bridge between the world and our God. Let us be like Hannah and turn to God in times of distress.

40

The Voice of God

TUESDAY, AUGUST 21, 2018

Seek his will in all you do, and he will
show you which path to take.
—Proverbs 3:6 (NLT)

Yesterday, as I left my home to travel to my workplace for the next two days, I wasn't in the most wonderful mood. Mondays are hard for me as I hit the road every week, traveling the roads and quite unsure of what I might find along the way. Most people probably would not be able to or want to work away from home, staying in strange towns. I have done this type of work several times and now remember how difficult it can be to be away from my husband for the majority of the week. However, I asked God for this position, and He granted it to me. The old saying goes, "Be careful what you ask for." God had quite a different way of reaching me yesterday, one that I never expected because I didn't choose to be completely quiet and listen to His voice.

As I left my driveway at home to travel to my workplace two hours away, I set my driving directions on my cell phone. I decided not to turn on my radio or make telephone calls along the way, as is my usual custom. I decided to follow the route that my GPS instructed instead of going the usual way to reach the interstate. I remembered that I had taken this route once or twice in the past, but it wasn't the way that I frequently traveled. The route that I took enabled me to travel on the back roads through the beautiful country with very little traffic. As I drove, God began to speak to me, and I heard Him clearly. It wasn't a booming voice from heaven as is often portrayed on movies and TV shows. It was a quiet voice that rang inside my mind. And as I asked questions, He began to answer me. When I asked how I might find money to purchase a property, He reminded me of when Jesus blessed the two fishes and five loaves of bread and was able to feed the five thousand. Nothing is impossible with God. We are what makes it impossible.

My entire drive to my workplace was stress free, peaceful, and joyful. I saw the beauty of God's world around me and didn't get caught up in the hustle and bustle of the traffic. The sense of peace gave me a mindset of calm, not anxiety. Most times, I get caught up in all the things that I need to do as I travel, like who I need to call, what I need to do when I get home, how this or that family member is doing. But this was not the case yesterday, and it was all the result of my being quiet and letting God lead the way. I loved being in communion with God. God has not changed from yesterday and will not change today or in the future. He is the same. He is our Father and wants to provide for us if only we are quiet and listen to His guidance. Christ has allowed us the opportunity to hear God. Christ sent the Holy Spirit to guide, direct, and comfort us at all times.

Throughout my teenage years and adulthood, my mother has often reminded me that I was a very quiet child. I had to take speech therapy because I couldn't speak clearly and didn't speak much at all. My older brother interpreted everything I said for others. My mother threw me a birthday party at the age of five to get me to quit saying, "Me wants" to do this or that. Most folks find it hard to believe that I was quiet, but I still struggle to pronounce some words. As I reflect on that time of life, I see that I enjoyed those years. I am beginning to remember, though, that I was in close communion with Jesus and God at that time in my life. The Spirit that dwells within enabled the communion.

I had begun to suspect that I had been with God in the past. Yesterday, it was made apparent through my conversation with God that I was with Him before I was even a thought in my mother's womb. We are all God's children, no matter our race, creed, or religion. We have all been created by our Father, who loves each and every one of us. We will always be children in God's eyes. May God enable you to be quiet and hear His tender voice.

41

The Womb of Mom

FRIDAY, NOVEMBER 22, 2019

> Yet you brought me safely from my
> mother's womb and led me to trust you
> at my mother's breast. I was thrust into
> your arms at my birth. You have been my
> God from the moment I was born.
> —Psalms 22:9–10 (NLT)

I imagine that I may type these journal notes to each of you until I can either no longer type or see or am too ill to do so. I find that this may not only assist you on your journey, but it assists me as well. You may decide to put these notes aside, but I hope that the Spirit will always draw you to read them, especially in times of uncertainty, trouble, and anguish but also in times of joy, happiness, and celebration. There is just something within me that drives me to continue with these notes. I feel as if I have found my passion and purpose in life after all my years of living.

Just as I reread this passage of scripture again this morning, verses 9–10 struck me even as I attended the funeral of my brother-in-law's father this past Wednesday. Even though my brother-in-law wanted a small funeral, the house was packed, as I expected. Workers from a local business were present at the gravesite as well as police officers and firefighters, as he had touched so many lives during his time on this earth. Funerals are not for the dead but for the living. I can imagine that even my brother-in-law's parents were viewing the funeral from above. It is most difficult, I think, when an only child loses parents, for they don't have a sibling to turn to. That is one of the reasons Jesus established the church on earth—so we will have many brothers and sisters in Christ standing by us in times of suffering, pain, and loss.

It is interesting that, in this passage of scripture, David mentions that God brought him safely from his mother's womb and that he was placed into God's arms at the moment of his birth. Even as a child struggles to be born, we adults struggle with dying. The prophet Jeremiah wrote, "I knew you before I formed you in your mother's womb" (1:5 NLT). All my years of living have finally led me to the conclusion that we were with God before we were in our mothers' wombs. I watched a movie the other day that perfectly shows that this may be possible. This movie gives clear insight into the struggles that a child goes through to be born. I have seen many mothers struggle to give birth to their children, even as I struggled to give birth to each of you. Even Mary, the mother of Jesus, struggled because God deemed it so when Adam and Eve where expelled from the Garden of Eden. God told Eve that she would have pain during childbirth. The beauty of it all, though, is that God erases the memory of the pain of childbirth. Not only is it a physical struggle for the mother to birth the child, but the child struggles to stay within the mother's womb for as long as possible. What do babies do the moment they are exposed to the atmosphere? Cry, of course—this tells the doctor and nurses that they are alive and well. The infants are immediately thrust into the mothers' arms for bonding, and God is there.

It is interesting that Psalm 23 follows the scripture discussed in this note. It was read at the funeral of my brother-in-law's father. In times of sorrow, it comforts family, and this scripture is there to give us comfort as well as we sojourn toward our heavenly home. It was written to give us peace when we struggle the most and don't know whether we can endure life and the sorrows that it brings. We know that David had a special place with God. God knew David before he was born. God knows all, even before it happens. He just watches and allows us to make our own decisions, just as we have to let our children make decisions on their own. We might think that we can control their lives, but we are gravely mistaken. What we can do is instill Christian values and provide guidance, sometimes from a distance, to assist them on their way home.

I know that God has allotted a specific time for each of us to return home. Many of us have faced death in our lives, and many of us didn't know whether we would make it through. My first experience came when I was five and my bike slid out from underneath me on a dirt road; an oncoming car was able to stop within inches of me. My guardian angel was there to stop that car. I have had experiences of near drownings too many times to count, car accidents, and physical abuse. Through it all, my guardian angel has fought for me. God has been near as I have struggled with anxiety, depression, financial losses, and much more. God has never left me; I have left Him but have found my way back into His loving arms. Just as David was placed in His arms at his birth, so I was placed into God's hands at my birth. Life is tough. The spiritual battle between good and evil exists, though hidden from our visual field. If we look closely, if we listen, if we get quiet, and if we follow our Lord and Savior, He will lead us safely home through the jungle of life, up and down the mountain trails, and on the waves of life. May the Lord bless and keep each of you safe, and may you be willing to get on the train that leads home.

42

Trials

SEPTEMBER 26, 2018

> Above all, you must realize that no prophecy
> in Scripture ever came from the prophet's own
> understanding, or from human initiative. No,
> those prophets were moved by the Holy Spirit,
> and they spoke from God.
> —2 Peter 1:20–21 (NLT)

I know that the verse above is truthful even as I type this note to you. The ideas, words, and scriptures that I type in each of my journal notes come from the Holy Spirit. This morning as I prepare to drive four hours today for the third day for work, I realize that I am weak, but God can make me strong if only I believe and allow Him to do so through Jesus Christ, my Lord and Savior. It's been a tough week so far, one in which I thought that I would be working by myself only to find out on my way to work that my boss sent me help. That help is from another coworker who had worked overtime the previous week by herself with no one to help her. With God's blessings, it is my belief that we will be finished right after the lunch hour, for both of us have a distance to drive.

My coworker asked for prayer for herself and her mother. Her mother was diagnosed with an incurable disease shortly after she took this job. That God puts in our minds the idea to take these positions has amazed me. I think that He knew that she would touch my life as I have touched hers.

It is wonderful to know without a doubt that God knows the future before we can even begin to think about it. If I had known in advance all the trials that I would lived though thus far, I doubt that I would have survived. It is true that God gives us only what we can handle. If I had not begun to choose to develop a stronger relationship with my Father, then life's burdens would have been too much. Our struggles make us grow. We can choose to either grow stronger in the faith or stronger in worldly desires. The world gives no hope of relief. Jesus gives us hope, love, comfort, companionship, and much more.

As I prepare to leave for work to undertake this drive, I know that Jesus is in the passenger seat. It's a wonderful relief to know that He sits there next to me. No, I don't understand it all, but I accept it for what it is. May you allow the Lord Jesus to come into your heart and direct your steps through life.

43

The Night Before Christmas

SUNDAY, DECEMBER 22, 2019

> You will find a baby, wrapped in swaddling
> cloths and lying in a manger.
> —Luke 2:12 (ESV)

I don't know why I am thinking of the poem "The Night Before Christmas" written by Clement Moore. It is not the night before Christmas, but maybe it is on my mind because my husband and I are sleeping in the basement of our house. I know that I was so excited as a child on Christmas Eve that it was amazing that I ever got any sleep. I was so excited to see what Santa had bought me for being a good girl all year long. "He knows when you are sleeping; he knows when you're awake; he knows if you've been bad or good, so be good for goodness' sake."[9] This is the first time that my husband and I have slept down here. Our little dog is so confused that I am awake, and by her actions I believe she is thinking that I am going to go up the stairs to our bedroom. This dog is so faithful to me. She gets up at any time that I may choose to wake up during the night.

It is so quiet after all the chaos of my granddaughter crying

---

[9] J. Fred Coots and Haven Gillespie, "Santa Claus Is Coming to Town," 1934.

because she didn't want to go to sleep. My husband snores softly in bed, which is separated from hers only by a single wall that doesn't have doors on either side of the room. It has been a wet and windy day; the wind continues to blow as I hear the wind chimes playing music constantly. The wind blows as if coming up an alley from the bottom of the yard—a wonderful sound—and the peace and calm that I sense at this very moment are wonderful. It is a new adventure even as my son's dogs sleep in the garage next door to this little apartment, which awaits someone to come and stay for short periods of time or even maybe a full-time tenant. Maybe sooner than later.

As the day of Christmas draws near, I am once again reminded that I am one of those late shoppers who drags their feet. Tomorrow morning is when I will be off to the local stores to retrieve the last few gifts. In all the hustle and bustle of this time of year, we need to remember the reason for the season—that God loved us so much that he sent His only Son to become human and dwell among us, knowing that His Son would eventually take it upon Himself to face the undignified death on a cross so that He would cover our sins with His blood, allowing us to come into communion with our heavenly Father. Jesus was a child born of a virgin mother, a young woman willing to accept the path that God had chosen for her. Jesus's human father was willing to take her as his wife despite the likely criticism and ridicule the young couple faced. They would raise this child of God, protect this child of God, and foster this child of God in the ways of the Lord. Mary would witness the abuse, mockery, beating, and eventual death of her child and then see the glory of God when this child was raised from the dead. She would understand that this would allow all who believed, accepted, and were willing to follow her child to have everlasting life.

I am reminded of the meaning of the circle, the greenery, and the candles on the advent wreath, a tradition that was started centuries ago in the early church. The circle represents God's unending love for us, while the greenery represents everlasting life. The candles symbolize north, south, east, and west, reaching out to all the corners of the world. The four red candles represent hope, peace, joy, and love. The white candle that is lit on Christmas Day represents the birthday of Christ, our Lord and Savior. Even as the little ones await the coming of Santa, we need to encourage them to understand the true meaning of Christmas by explaining the real reason for the season through the use of nativity sets in our homes. We should allow them to tell the story to us as adults and touch the figures in the set—the angel, the shepherds, the lamb, the cow, the wise men, Mary and Joseph, and most importantly, the baby Jesus.

May the Lord be with you and yours tonight, tomorrow night, and every night. Good night.

44

Unexpected

SUNDAY, DECEMBER 17, 2017

But blessed are those who trust in the Lord and
have made the Lord their hope and confidence.
—Jeremiah 17:7 (NLT)

Yesterday I received something unexpected in the mail. The prior
week I had decided to send my tithe, which was well overdue, to
the Lord. Even though my financial resources were low, I trusted
that God would take care of us. I was expecting a refund check
from a company; however, I didn't expect that I would receive
two additional refund checks that amounted to double what I had
tithed. God had blessed me twofold. These unexpected blessings
that happen to us need to be declared for what they are, blessings
from God.

Unexpected blessings don't have to be financial. They can be as
simple as knowing within your being that the sun is needed during
the rain, and the Lord sends a ray of sunshine to warm your soul. It
could be a blooming flower that pops above the snow. It could be
the giggle of a laughing child that lifts your soul from depression.
Unexpected blessings many times escape our vision for we are so
caught up in the many "things" around us. As a nurse, I assess

patients from head to toe to look for the unexpected problems, but if I didn't listen to my patient, then I would miss some. Nursing is about listening to and observing the patient; it is not just putting our trust in machines. I thank God that, through my years in the nursing profession, He has taught me to observe and listen.

Look for the unexpected blessings that God sends you each and every day. Look for those little moments in which you begin to discover things in the way that small children explore the world around them. Watch that child as the child watches the movement of a small creature, such as an ant. Watch as children interact with animals around them and the joy that they experience, evident in their laughter. Watch as children begin to create a chalk drawing on concrete and observe their concentration. Visit with elderly family members and see the smiles that come across their faces and the joy that is expressed in their words. Take time to be with our Lord and begin to realize that God has opened your eyes in ways that you can't understand. Recognize and thank Him for the unexpected blessing of beginning to understand what is written in His Word.

If you are blessed with the unexpected, bless others as well. "When someone has been given much, much will be required in return; and when someone has been entrusted with much, even more will be required" (Luke 12:48 NLT).

45

What a Day of Rejoicing

FRIDAY, OCTOBER 12, 2018

Whoever has the Son has life; whoever does not
have God's Son does not have life.… And we are
confident that he hears us whenever we ask for
anything that pleases him. And since we know
he hears us when we make our requests, we also
know that he will give us what we ask for.… We
know that God's children do not make a practice
of sinning, for God's Son holds them securely, and
the evil one cannot touch them. We know that we
are children of God and that the world around us
is under the control of the evil one. And we know
that the Son of God has come, and he has given
us understanding so that we can know the true
God.… Dear children, keep away from anything
that might take God's place in your hearts.
—1 John 5:12, 14–15, 18–20, 21 (NLT)

I sit in my study as the light of a new day is on the horizon. I have
taken time to read, study, and ponder the words in the Good Book
that help me to understand and strengthen my faith in my Lord,

Jesus Christ. I think about my children and my grandbaby as they sleep in the guest rooms. I lit a candle this morning, but I noticed that it was barely burning. I tilted the jar, and the flame caught onto the wax in the jar, resulting in a full flame. It reminded me of the verse, "Let your light so shine before men that they may see your good works, and glorify your Father which is in heaven" (Matthew 5:16 NKJV). The light takes away the darkness, and the darkness cannot overcome the light.

It is a beautiful morning as the birds begin to sing praises to our Maker and Creator, feeling the coolness and calmness in the air as the storm has passed. It is a new day with new opportunities to grow in this life and follow the light. The darkness of this world makes us think that the evil one has control, but God, the Father; Christ, the Son; and the Holy Ghost overpower this world and the evil one. The day is coming when the evil one will be destroyed once and forever. That is why it is important not to conform to this world but to be transformed by the renewing of one's mind. Clearly, the devil and demons want to control our minds. As children of God, we are provided protection. That seems difficult to understand unless we really study and explore the scriptures. The Holy Spirit will lead us to understand the truth. Christ came to deliver us from our evil ways, to become victorious over death and the grave, and to allow us to come into the presence of God.

I don't understand everything, but I do know that the more that I study, think, trust, and ask for guidance, the more that is revealed to me. I must listen too, for God, Christ, and the Spirit do not speak in loud voices. Listening is very difficult for me. I want to formulate my response to people while they are still trying to communicate their thoughts to me. If I can learn to be quiet again, as I once was as a child, then I will hear the voice of God, Christ, and the Holy Spirit. Sometimes, it is Christ that I hear; sometimes God; and so many times, I feel the Holy Spirit working from within my heart. When I am in the protection of Christ, I sense that evil is kept at bay.

As I listen to my children talk about their difficulties, I have come to realize that the most powerful thing I can do is to pray for them. God protects His children through requests made in Jesus's name. As I face surgery in a few weeks to replace a knee joint, I trust that God, Christ, and the Holy Spirit will protect me. Last week, as I talked with another Christian about my surgery, he told me that this is God's time to spend with me. What a thought! God wants to spend time just with me and no one else during this time. Our God is a powerful, almighty God quite capable of being with all His children at the same time. Our finite minds do not allow us to comprehend the magnitude of our Father. One day, though, we will be gathered by the Good Shepherd and taken to dwell within the fold forever.

"What a day of rejoicing that will be, when we all see Jesus we'll sing and shout the victory." May the Lord bless you and yours and keep you safe today, tomorrow, and always.

46

Where Were You?

TUESDAY, SEPTEMBER 11, 2018

Listen! The armies of many nations roar like the
roaring of the sea. Hear the thunder of the mighty
forces as they rush forward like thundering waves.
But though they thunder like breakers on a beach,
God will silence them, and they will run away.
—Isaiah 17:12–13 (NLT)

Where were you on September 11, 2001? Some of you were not even
a thought in your mothers' minds. Some of you were children, some
were young adults, some were middle age or older, and some are no
longer with us. I remember where I was and what was going on that
day. I was on my way to work when I received a telephone call from
my coworker saying that a plane had hit one of the towers in New
York. We thought that it was an accident. It was only when I received
a second call from my coworker, saying that another plane had hit
the second tower, that we realized that the country was under attack.

I stood in a large hospital lobby when the second tower fell. As I
stood next to a doctor, I said, "They have no regard for human life."
Looking back, I don't remember feeling fearful, just concerned. I
had already been through quite a lot, being recently separated from

my husband. I was in charge and responsible for three children. I had to make the decisions regarding their security. I remember my coworker saying to me, "Go home, fill up your car with a tank of gas, and pull some cash out of your bank." None of us knew the impact this attack would have on our country.

For weeks, the TV stations broadcasted events from the attack. Not only were the Twin Towers in New York struck but the Pentagon was too, and a plane was brought down in a field in Pennsylvania by heroes to prevent further damage. The plane that crashed in Pennsylvania was headed for the White House. The president just happened to be in a town near where I lived, reading to schoolchildren in a local elementary school. The moment he was told was captured on video, and the expression on his face immediately changed.

Beyond this tragedy, the town in which I lived was hit by a tropical depression that caused a power outage and flooding for three days. I was recently separated from my husband, and America was under attack, I was facing a tropical depression, and I had three children for whom I was responsible. Seventeen years later, I have survived through the grace and mercy of God, Christ, and the Holy Spirit.

I am quite fortunate this year in that I am able to type this note in my home study this morning. I have had a very difficult year since I returned to work. I have dealt with a sick father, a sick mother, a sick husband, the death of my mother-in-law, the early births of two grandchildren, and upcoming knee surgery for myself. Last night I went to my parents' house to provide a treatment for my elderly father, which wore me out because I had returned from work so late. God is with me, Christ is with me, and the Holy Spirit is with me. This provides me with assurance that the Trinity will be with me as I face the future. God has always taken care of me and will continue to do so, if only I continue to believe.

May you reflect on where you were seventeen years ago. Never forget, and never forget the love and mercy of our God, our Father. May He bless you and yours through His Son, Jesus Christ, and may the Holy Spirit give you comfort.

47

Wonder

THURSDAY, DECEMBER 19, 2019

> For a child is born to us, a son is given to us.
> The government will rest on his shoulders. And
> he will be called Wonderful Counselor, Mighty
> God, Everlasting Father, Prince of Peace.
> —Isaiah 9:6 (NLT)

There is something wonderful about sitting in the dark with just the lights on the Christmas tree ablaze in the colors of green, pink, blue, and orange. These colors are more muted than the stark light that beams forth from white lights. A single angel sits atop the tree holding two white lights that represent candles in each hand, looking down from above the tree. This angel announces the birth of Christ the Lord.

This scene reminds me of years past when I was a small child. I would sit in front of the Christmas tree in the one room dedicated each year as the one to house the tree. The living room was special, as it was only used on special occasions. It served as a place of retreat and quiet, especially during my Christmas visits at night. I would sit on the floor under the tree and dream about whether Santa would bring me the toys that I wished for that year. I might even hear the voices of singing on the radio in the distance. A sense of peace and calm would overtake me.

I knew, though, from an early age that Christmas was more about Christ than Santa. I would participate in Christmas church plays and eventually direct church pageants as a young mother—a time of wonder and mystery for all who would take the time to relish in the scene. I relish this early morning, a new day, in this scene once more as the rest of the household sleeps. Instead of hearing the voices singing across the radio, I now hear snoring in the distance. It's a blessing, for it tells me that the person lives and that I can still hear the sound at my age. Again, a sense of peace and calm overshadows me and gives me peace.

The wonderment that a child feels at Christmas can also be felt as adults if only we allow it to be so, if only we make a special time each and every day to come into the presence of God and to look up more than we look down. We can feel this wonder if only we understand the importance of worship to the newborn King. Christ is not just for Christmas but for each month, day, hour, minute, and second of the year. That wonderment gives us the peace and calm that we need on a daily basis. It guides us along the path toward our heavenly home. He at times holds our hands, picks us up, and even carries us when we are too weak and weary and too overburdened with the trials of this world. He is our Counselor, Mighty Father, Everlasting Father, and Prince of Peace.

May your time with Christ remind you of the love of God for each of His children and that He does provide peace that never ends.

48

Work and Play

TUESDAY, FEBRUARY 4, 2020

> As for every man to whom God has given
> riches and wealth, and given him power to eat
> of it, to receive his heritage and rejoice in his
> labor—this is the gift of God. For he will not
> dwell unduly on the days of his life, because
> God keeps him busy with the joy of his heart.
> —Ecclesiastes 6:19–20 (NKJV)

I think of my husband this morning as I type this note. He will be coming back to our house this morning because we have another couple interested in possibly renting this house for a year. I trust that God will send us the right family to rent this home, as my husband's next project is to update his family home. I know that his parents in heaven are aware of what he is undertaking and are proud of him. We are looking outside the box and using our investments to work for us. I have finally realized that job opportunities are slim because of my age. I remember addressing the issue of stereotypes on aging while writing a paper for an independent graduate study course back in the late 1970s. These same stereotypes exist today. We are living longer, but much has not changed.

I know that God provided us the vision to think outside the box to work together. I also know that my husband's God-given talent and love is in building and renovating homes. I know that it gives him pleasure to create environments for others to enjoy. As we age, we can focus too much on what we can't do now instead of focusing on what we can do with God's help. God has put many thoughts and visions in my mind, and I trust that they will happen.

God will keep my husband busy with the joy of his heart. God may even give my dad pleasure to watch the process. I always am looking out for others, but that's OK too, for that is how God created me. I receive my greatest joy from helping others. I REALLY am a nurse; I have always wanted to be a nurse since I was a little girl. Revelations come at unexpected times, just as now. My time of helping others, though, I feel is in my notes to you to read years down the road. This is my gift to each of you. We don't live long on this earth but are just passing though. We need to leave this world better than we may have found it. We need to tell others about the way home so that they can join us. Our home is not limited to just a few but is available to all God's children.

Printed in the United States
by Baker & Taylor Publisher Services